LIKE
A THIEF

What the Bible Really Says
About End Times

Samuel King

Connect with us:

Walking in the Word Ministries Inc.

(Like us on Facebook)

Cover: Nicole Goodhue Designs

Cover Photography: Sepavo / 123RF Stock Photo, FreeImages.com

Dedication

My heartfelt thanks to my wife, Judith, and our three children for their love, encouragement and support.

CONTENTS

PART I: THE FIRST COMING OF CHRIST

PART II THE SECOND COMING OF CHRIST

Part I:

The First Coming of Christ

CHAPTER 1

STARTING ON THE RIGHT FOOT!

I t is an early Friday morning in late July. As I look out of my office window, I see the beautiful lawn and lush woods after an overnight downpour. It is here I usually experience quiet refreshing with the Lord.

On this particular morning, I have a great deal on my mind and heart. I pastor a growing congregation in central Virginia. The burdens of my parishioners sometimes seem overwhelming. I am married to a beautiful woman and we have been blessed with three great kids. Our oldest daughter has graduated from college and lives in New York City. Our son is in his second year of college and our youngest daughter leaves for her first year of university life in two weeks.

As you can imagine, my life is extremely busy. The temptation to worry raises its ugly head. Just as that temptation is about to overtake me, I see through my window a beautiful robin feeding from the grass behind our church. I am vividly reminded, one more time, of Jesus' words in Mathew 6:26,

"Look at the birds of the air, they do not sow
or reap or store away in barns, and yet your
heavenly Father feeds them. Are you not much
more valuable than they?" (NIV)

In this hectic, "break neck" pace of the information age, one can easily lose sight of the wonderful, loving care the Creator gives His creation. Personal and family issues, career and job insecurities, or just making ends meet, can stress us to the max. Not to mention societal and global crises such as crime, failure of our educational systems, safety of our streets, nuclear threat of the Middle East, earthquakes, natural disasters, and of course, the ever-present war on terrorism. With this world seemingly spiraling out of control, where do we go for help, relief, and comfort? In whom do we trust for our future and our children's future? Do we dare sit back and do nothing except leave our futures to the "experts" to figure out? Do we just work at our jobs day-to-day, week to week and year to year in hopes that everything will work itself out for the best? What does the future hold for our family, friends, country and world? Is there anyone out there who can help us with all the pressing issues of our generation?

I am not a prophet, nor the son of one – yet there is Truth all around staring us in the face. Truth? Where in the world do we or should we look for truth? In the pages ahead it is my sincere hope to share the Truth of what the Creator has in store for you and me – His created. Before we go there, we must clarify a few vital and most important foundational points.

What Is Your Worldview?

A term today that "is tossed about" quite often is "world view". If I were to ask you, "What is your world view?" Basically, I would be asking, "What is your philosophy?" or "What is your view of life?" One's philosophy or worldview would consist of the accumulation of information, be it true or false, which would influence our opinions on the topics of life. Allow me to ask you a personal question – "What is the basis of your world view?" Education, environment, experiences and how we were raised are some factors that influence our thinking and formulation of our opinions. Again, "What is the basis of your thinking, beliefs, values and the way you live your life?"

For you to receive the maximum benefit from reading this book, we need to establish a basis of understanding. When I was a boy there was a popular afternoon television program called "To Tell the Truth". Man, I loved that show. Each one opened with the curtain being raised and three individuals all saying the same name. The moderator would read the true person's story. Then it was up to the panel of guests, the studio audience and those watching to determine who was really telling the truth.

Life is too often like that T.V. show. We have competing voices (worldviews) constantly vying for our attention and allegiance. Which ones are false? Which one is true? Does truth come solely from the Roman Catholic Church? What's the true story on all the denominations? Are the Jehovah's Witnesses the true ones? What about Joseph Smith and the Mormons – have they got truth? What's the deal with Scientology that many of our Hollywood darlings are now espousing? Are the world's major religions – Islam, Hinduism, Judaism, Buddhism, secular humanism all true? Do they all lead us to peace, prosperity and heaven? Are we looking to Captain Kirk, Dr. Spock and the crew of the Enterprise for our deliverance? That last one may be too fictitious, yet look around – much of the world's population trusts only in things they can see and feel – creeds, rituals, idols – things that are made by the hands of man. Yet, I submit to you again – Truth is all around us – the Truth is staring us in the eye.

So Who Is Jesus, Really?

Have you ever asked yourself, "Who really is Jesus?" Like the T.V. show "To Tell the Truth", would the real Jesus please stand up? According to your worldview, you already have assessed the situation. Your mind, based on what evidence you have, has already made a determination. What is the basis of your view of who Jesus Christ truly is? Did you form your opinion from your parents' views? T.V. preachers? Today's media? Today's educational system? Pop culture? The guys at work? I could go on, but enough – you are an intelligent human being – you get the point.

Let's take a few moments to explore this question of exactly who Jesus Christ is? First of all, we know that he is a historical figure – a living person. The historical writings, be they Jewish or Gentile, tell of a man named Jesus of Nazareth. He was born in Bethlehem in the first century A.D. He lived most of his earthly life in Nazareth as a carpenter; son of a Jewish couple named Joseph and Mary. Jesus was the oldest child in his family and had several younger half brothers and sisters. At about age thirty he left his hometown, his family and his job to begin a public ministry as an itinerant teacher. Most of this information can be found in non-biblical, historical documents. What I mean by "non-biblical" is writings that are true and reliable, yet are found outside of scripture. It has been said by scholars and historians that more has been written about Jesus Christ than any other person in human history. I encourage you to explore what men and women (outside of the biblical writings) have had to say about Jesus through the centuries. Yet, in the grand scheme of things, it is not so much of what they say about him – but rather what you believe about the "Son of Man"? Jesus phrased this question of his own disciples by asking them, "Who do you say that I am?"

As a pastor, I have counseled many people through the years. Most of them had very serious problems. It may have been a problem with relationships, financial stress and, or personal habits. Whatever their need was – when we together would go to God in prayer and seek Him in His Word – He would always deliver. He is faithful to meet our needs. Why? Because God loves you and desires intimate friendship with you!

Any information I would share with you would be totally incomplete without seeking out or searching the Scriptures. **What does the Bible say about God; about Jesus; about his first Advent and his Second Coming?**

Before we go further concerning some of what the Bible teaches about these topics, we must clarify our thinking. Primarily, what is your view of the Bible? Do you see it as merely an ancient book? Does it just sit on your coffee table collecting dust? Or do you see it as the Holy, inspired, inerrant Word of God?

Amazing Facts About God's Word, the Bible

The sixty-six books of the Bible were written over a thirty-four hundred-year time span by thirty different writers! Yet, one all-encompassing truth continues to burn brighter with each passing day. God inspired each biblical writer for one very large, eternal purpose -- to draw you to Himself! From Genesis to Revelation, God uses those willing vessels to shed light that His highest creation – human beings - would come to know Him!

As we look into the Bible, you may still be hesitant – thinking perhaps, is it true, reliable, or trustworthy? I encourage you to discover the answers for yourself. As Paul wrote to Timothy in II Timothy 3:16,17:

"All Scripture is God-breathed and is useful for teaching, rebuking, correcting and training in righteousness, so that the man of God may be thoroughly equipped for every good work".

However, you nor I nor anyone else will discover much about God's Word without first picking it up and making a whole-hearted commitment to studying it. I challenge you to be a Berean! Paul spoke of the Bereans in Acts 17:11,

"Now the Bereans were of more noble character than the Thessalonians, for they received the message with great eagerness and examined the Scriptures every day to see if what Paul said was true".

This is my hope for you and every believer on the planet – that you would examine the Word daily and the answers to life's most difficult questions will be yours.

Don't Just Take My Word For It

Anything I write in this book, please – I sincerely urge you to check it out! Do not just take my word for it – search the Scriptures each day for yourself. The Book of Proverbs comes to my mind, Proverbs 27:17 says,

"As iron sharpens iron so one man sharpens another".

My heartfelt prayer is that this book will help sharpen and alert you to some of the awesome things God has in store for you!

As we begin to examine the Bible and explore the question, "Who is Jesus Christ?" there is one vitally important truth we cannot and must not ignore -- allowing Scripture to interpret Scripture. What that means is that for one to gain the true meaning or meanings of the teachings of God, we must use Biblical truths to shed light on other Biblical principles. In other words, we compare and contrast God's instruction in the Old Testament with the teachings of the New Testament and vice versa. We evaluate what Jesus taught with the teachings of Moses, the prophets, the apostles and so on. Thus, we gain clearer understanding of what God desires to teach us. In studying prophecy, we will use this important method to receive the plain, simple truth concerning future events.

Bible commentaries, concordances, dictionaries and many other study aids are wonderful resources. Yet, we must hold to this truth – to receive the true meaning of the text, we compare Scripture to Scripture. Learning about the writer, the time of history in which he or she lived, the writer's audience or recipients, and the reason for the writing are all valid points to research. Yet, Jesus said in Matthew 24:35,

> *"Heaven and earth will pass away, but my*
> *words will never pass away".*

Therefore, we can see from this text and II Timothy 3:16, 17 that Jesus' words or teachings are reliable, truthful and trustworthy!

In this same Matthew 24 passage, Jesus warned,

> *"Watch out that no one deceives you. For*
> *many will come in my name, claiming "I am*
> *the Christ (or Messiah)", and will deceive*
> *many"* (Matthew 24:4-5 NIV).

It has been God's plan from the beginning, starting with Adam and Eve – to reveal Himself to mankind. In the Book of Genesis, we see God walking with man daily. Our Creator desires for all people to know the truth. Jesus said, "You will know the truth and the truth will set you free." Free to do what? Free to have a relationship with him. God has used the Bible to explain what He has done in the past. He also speaks through the prophets to tell us what we can expect in the future. Thus, He uses prophecy to show us the truth concerning Jesus' first coming and He uses prophecy to show us the truth about his Second Coming!

Cult or Christ?

The twentieth century landscape is littered with cults, dictatorships, false teachings and individuals claiming to be God,

God's Son, or a messenger from God. People like Hitler, Stalin, Lenin, Jim Jones, David Koresh, and the Mahareshi Yogi are just a few examples. False teachings of Mormonism, Jehovah's Witnesses, and Scientology are all on the rise – gaining new converts each day. As stated earlier, all of these philosophies, religions or worldviews may contain some truth – but can they all be true? When comparing any thoughts, philosophies or religions to Jesus' teachings, we must examine what Jesus said about himself. While the world and its views clamor, even demand our attention – John 14:6 stands above all the rest. Speaking in this verse, Jesus said,

> *"I am the way and the truth and the life. No one comes to the Father except through me".*

Thus, we begin our journey of discovering Truth. It is my hope that you will see that truth is not a view; it is not relative, it is not a concept – Truth is a person!

CHAPTER 2

WHEN TRUTH BECAME A PERSON: THE ADVENT

OF JESUS CHRIST

For us to gain understanding about the Second Coming of Christ, we must have a solid foundation of truth concerning his first arrival. As stated in the previous chapter, historical documents abound concerning Jesus the man. The Jewish writers Josephus and Eusebius, record what first century Jewish life was like under Roman rule and occupation. These men give the world information concerning Jesus, his family, his teaching ministry and his excruciating death on a Roman cross.

One question we, as believers or seekers, need to explore is "Why did Jesus Christ come to earth?" Why was he born? One answer is found in John 3:16-18,

> *"For God so loved the world that He gave his one and only Son, that whoever believes in him shall not perish but have eternal life. For God did not send his Son to the world to condemn*

the world, but to save the world through him. Whoever believes in him is not condemned, but whoever does not believe stands condemned already because he has not believed in the name of God's one and only Son" (NIV).

In this short passage we find God's plan of salvation revealed to mankind. In Romans 3:22-23, Paul writes,

"This righteousness from God comes through faith in Jesus Christ to all who believe. There is no difference, for all have sinned and fallen short of the glory of God."

Here, we are practicing a most important principle – using scripture to interpret scripture - thus, gaining clearer understanding on one of the great questions of life – "How can I get to Heaven?"

So Why Do We Need a Savior?

Let's examine some of the truths of these two passages. First, the Romans chapter three verses tell us why we need a Savior. All of humanity from Adam on down to the newest baby being born today "falls short of the glory of God". Our sin separates us from our holy God. For you and me to experience true fellowship/relationship with the Creator, we must have our sins cleansed and forgiven. The true

Lord God Almighty – creator of the entire universe – is perfect, sinless, and changeless.

> *"God is light; in Him there is no darkness at all"* (1 John 1:5).

Therefore, we must have our sin or darkness "issue" resolved.

What is the Character of God?

As we look into the passage in John, we see some revealing truths about the character of God. First, He is a Father. He has a Son, a one and only Son whose name is Jesus Christ. Secondly, God is love – "for God so loved the world (people – humanity) that He gave His only Son." Romans 5:8 states,

> *"But God demonstrates his own love for us in this: While we were still sinners, Christ died for us."*

The true and living Lord does not demand that we go out and kill others or die for him to obtain or receive salvation. He is the one who came to die for us. We are not to shed other's blood to prove our love and devotion to him. It is he who proved once and for all his love and devotion for us by giving himself on the cross. Do not allow the false religions of the world to deceive you. Always – I mean **always** – run their claims, doctrines and teachings through God's Word first and allow the Holy Spirit to lead you and guide you to

Truth. Then it will be very clear as to whether their teachings are true or false. John writes in 1John 1:6-10,

> *"If we claim to have fellowship with him yet walk in darkness, we lie and do not live by the truth. But if we walk in the light, as He is in the light, we have fellowship (relationship) with one another, and the blood of Jesus, his Son, purifies us from all sin. If we claim to be without sin, we deceive ourselves and the truth is not in us. If we confess our sins, He is faithful and just and will forgive us our sins and purify us from all unrighteousness. If we claim we have not sinned, we make him out to be a liar and his word has no place in our lives"* (NIV).

It is clear from this passage that God sincerely desires a relationship with His created – mankind. He has gone to incredible lengths to prove His love for us, and He desires to relate to us as a loving, giving, generous Father.

What Was Special About Christ's Birth?

A second question that needs addressing is concerning his miraculous birth. The prophets predicted his birth centuries before it happened. Isaiah chapter 7:14 says,

"Therefore the Lord himself will give you a sign: The virgin will be with child and will give birth to a son, and will call him Immanuel."

Two important points about this – first, the word "you" in the first part of the sentence is plural in the Hebrew, meaning the Lord himself will give a sign to *you* – the nation of Israel and the entire world! The sign being a miraculous birth – a virgin (one who has never had sexual relations with a man) is going to give birth to a male child and call him Immanuel, which means "God with us." This is a huge prophetic statement made by a Jewish prophet almost *seven hundred years before Jesus was born*! God wanted no one to miss this promise, as the name Isaiah means "The Lord saves." The prophet whose name means "The Lord saves" is the very one given the prophetic word of the birth of the one, Jesus, whose name *also* means, "The Lord Saves!" And capitalizing "The" in the phrase "The Lord saves" is exactly correct as our God wants all to know that salvation comes only from the true, living Holy One of Israel! This salvation comes only through God's one and only Son – "*The* Lord Jesus Christ."

Looking in chapter one of Matthew's Gospel we see confirmation of Isaiah 7:14. Matthew lists the genealogy of Jesus from his "earthly father," Joseph; all the way back through Solomon, David ... Boaz and Ruth, Judah, Jacob, Isaac, and Abraham. He tells briefly of Joseph's concern, as his fiancé was pregnant and Joseph knew the baby was not his! Certainly this was cause for alarm – particularly in those days! Matthew 1:19-25 explains how God answered Joseph's concern by using an angel in a dream to reassure him about Mary and the virgin birth. Joseph was thinking of quietly divorcing Mary (verse 19). God intervenes by sending His messenger that speaks to Joseph in a dream. The angel addresses him by saying,

> *"Joseph, son of David, do not be afraid to take Mary home as your wife, because what is conceived in her is from the Holy Spirit. She will give birth to a son, and you are to give him the name Jesus, because he will save his people from their sins."*

Here, Matthew connects this heavenly message to Isaiah 7:14,

> *"All this took place to fulfill what the Lord had said through the prophet (Isaiah): The virgin will be with child and will give birth to a son, and they will call him Immanuel, which means, "God with us."*

In verse 24, Joseph obeys:

"When Joseph woke up, he did what the angel of the Lord commanded him and took Mary home as his wife."

In verse 25, Joseph demonstrates his integrity by not having sex with his wife until after the baby is born. This one fact greatly supports the truth concerning the virgin birth of Jesus Christ,

"But he had no union with her until she gave birth to a son. And he gave him the name Jesus."

Is our God amazing or what? Thank God for His Word that shares with us the Truth concerning His plan of salvation for all who will believe. This is just one of the more than 200 prophecies that refer to the Messiah's coming. The first is found in Isaiah 9:6-7a,

"For unto us a child is born, to us a son is given, and the government will be on his shoulders. And he will be called Wonderful Counselor, Mighty God, Everlasting Father, and Prince of Peace. Of the increase of his government and peace there will be no end."

Another Messianic prophecy is found in Psalm 110. God's covenant with King David states that one from his royal lineage would rule forever, which is fulfilled in the person of Jesus Christ. Verse 4 reads,

> *"The Lord has sworn and will not change his mind: "You are a priest forever, in the order of Melchizedek."*

Isaiah 16:5 supports this theme,

> *"In love a throne will be established; in faithfulness a man will sit on it – one from the house of David – who in judging seeks justice and speeds the cause of righteousness."*

Jeremiah 33:16; Isaiah 40:3-5; Zechariah 3:8, 9:9-10, all point to the Messiah – Jesus Christ! Let's move on to see what Luke has to say about this issue of a virgin birth.

Luke Speaks Out About Christ's Birth

Virgin birth? How can that be? Is it possible? Let's examine the story in the Gospel of Luke chapter 1:26-38. In verses 26-28, God sends the angel Gabriel to a virgin named Mary to let her know that she is, "highly favored." So favored that the Lord has chosen her to give birth to His Son (vs. 30-31). Gabriel goes on to say,

> *"You are to name him Jesus...He will be called Son of the most High...He will reign over the*

> *house of Jacob and his kingdom will never*
> *end."*

Mary struggles to take in all this awesome news. She asks the angel a most important question in verse 34,

> *"How will this be, since I am a virgin?"*

Gabriel responds with comforting words,

> *"The Holy Spirit will come upon you, and the*
> *power of Most High will overshadow you. So*
> *the Holy One to be born will be called the Son*
> *of God... For nothing is impossible with God."*

With her concerns answered, Mary agrees to obey God's request.

What an incredible story! Here we have just a few of the most important facts about the birth of Jesus – yet, something – something seems to be missing. Could the missing element be faith? Do you *believe* in the "virgin birth" of Jesus Christ? There was a popular television police show years ago, and the detective, when investigating, when looking for evidence, would often say, "Just the Facts, Ma'am." This perspective is so representative of our society today. Many people claim to want the truth, the facts, the straight-scoop, yet when the Lord God – Creator of the universe – gives them the Truth, many would prefer a different version! These are the same people who choose to believe in Darwinism (with little or no evidence), - who put their faith in technology, money, government, or the United Nations – all of which have failed! Yet, sadly these same people reject the Truth from the One who CANNOT FAIL.

Where Would He Be Born?

I want to investigate and explore one last question of Jesus' earthly beginnings. Where was his birth to take place? You would think that if God was sending His Son into the world to accomplish the Father's purpose – He would announce where this deliverer would be born! God does better than that – He speaks through the prophet Micah. Micah chapter five, beginning in verse two:

"But you, Bethlehem Ephrathah, though you are small among the clans (rulers) of Judah, out of you will come for me one who will be ruler over Israel, whose origins are from of old, from ancient times. Therefore, Israel will be abandoned until the time when she who is in labor gives birth, and the rest of his brothers return to join the Israelites. He will stand and shepherd his flock in the strength of the Lord, in the majesty of the name of the Lord his God. And they will live securely, for then his greatness will reach to the ends of the

earth. And he will be their peace" (Micah 5:2-
5a NIV).

Starting in verse 2, we see that God announces the birthplace
of Messiah will be Bethlehem, Ephrathah. The Lord was so specific
that He includes the term "Ephrathah", which is the larger region in
which the town Bethlehem was located. Today, when we want to
specify the exact location of a town or city we use the city, state and
even the zip code. The Creator desired that no one would miss this
prophetic message concerning Messiah's place of birth – thus He
specifies the **exact location** – town and region where Jesus was to
be born! What an awesome God!

Still in verse 2, the phrase *"small among the clans of Judah"*
allows the reader further confidence in Jesus Christ as Messiah
because Jesus' earthly lineage or heritage is from the tribe of Judah!
The phrase, *"out of you will come for me one who will be ruler over
Israel, whose origins are from of old, from ancient times,"* should not
confuse us at all – if we will use scripture to interpret scripture. In
John 8:56-58 we read:

> *"Your father Abraham rejoiced at the thought
> of seeing my day; he saw it and was glad.' 'You
> are not yet fifty years old,' the Jews said to
> him, 'and you have seen Abraham!' 'I tell you
> the truth,' Jesus answered, 'Before Abraham
> was born, I am!' "*

21

In this scene, the Jews are disputing with Jesus concerning his teachings. Jesus shares with them that they may be physically related to Abraham, but by their actions and accusations they are not spiritually related to Abraham at all. In verse 56, Jesus says that Abraham rejoiced at the very thought of seeing Jesus' day and when Abraham saw it he was glad. The Jews, in verse 57 make the obvious observation that chronologically it would be impossible for Jesus to have seen Abraham. Jesus, in verse 58, responds,

> "I tell you the truth before Abraham was born,
> I am!"

Here Jesus is stating the truth concerning his divinity as the Son of God and expressing his oneness with the Father. Affirming also, by this solemn, emphatic oath, Jesus' connection with the Father, which represents God instructing Moses to tell the Israelites that, "*I AM has sent me to you*," (Exodus 3:14 NIV). Just as the Father sent Moses to deliver the nation of Israel[1], God the Father now sends God the Son to deliver Israel and all the nations!

How Can We Know Jesus is the True Messiah?

This Micah passage is huge in identifying Christ Jesus as Messiah. Verse 3 speaks of Israel being abandoned because of her idolatry and worship of false gods. That is, until Messiah is born! The time that elapsed from Malachi, the last book in the Old Testament, to the birth of Christ and the beginning of the New Testament was four hundred years! God is very serious about His people obeying His Word.

The second part of verse 3 shifts gears. No longer is Micah speaking of Messiah's birth – he is now prophesying further into the future about the Messianic reign when Messiah (Jesus) rules all the nations on planet earth. One important fact to note as we study prophecy: we must consider the short-term aspect and the long-term aspect of the spoken words. Whether it is Isaiah, Jeremiah, Micah, or whoever the biblical prophet may be, we must use scripture to explain (interpret) scripture. And, as in verse 3, the scene may shift quickly and dramatically without warning. Verses 3a-5a speak of the Messianic rule ... "the rest of his brothers return to join the Israelites" which means all true believers joining Jesus to "rule and reign" with him.

What Exactly is Prophecy?

Let's take a moment to clarify the biblical term "prophecy." Prophecy is defined as "A communication of the mind of God imparted to a believer by the Holy Spirit. It may be a prediction or an indication of the will of God in a given situation" 1 (NIV study note). Thus, those with the gift of prophecy, regardless whether the person is an Old Testament or New Testament prophet, are given this "spiritual gift" by God to help strengthen His people. No other religion, cult or worldview possesses the "gift of prophecy." Secular Humanism, where the individual is his/her own god, has no prophecy. Islam also rejects the God of the Bible and seeks its own violent version of future predictions. Judaism is incomplete since Messiah and the prophets who wrote of him were emphatically rejected.

> *"Taze Russell, founder of Jehovah Witnesses, is not a true prophet as all of his predictions concerning Jesus' Second Coming proved false. Joseph Smith, founder of Mormonism, is also a false prophet as his teachings and predictions have been edited and modified thousands of times"* 2 (Cults, False Religions – Josh Mc Dowell).

As we finish this passage from Micah, verses 4 and 5 are a beautiful word depiction of the Good Shepherd tending his flock "in the strength ... majesty ... and name of the Lord his God. And they will live securely, for then his greatness will reach to the ends of the earth. And he will be their peace."

This "time" or "age" has obviously not taken place yet; it is a direct reference to the earthly rule of Christ that closes out human history. The Hebrew word for "peace" (shalom) gives a picture of a time of prosperity, security, and peace like man has never known. This peace, security, and prosperity will be lasting. Why? Because it is rooted in God - NOT man! The prophet Daniel saw in his vision the four great earthly kingdoms all rising and all four falling into the dust. Yet, then he saw the Kingdom of ... *"one like a son of man..."* whose dominion is an everlasting dominion that will not pass away, whose kingdom is one that will never be destroyed. (Daniel 7:13-14, NIV).

In our next chapter we will explore the title Jesus gave himself – "Son of Man." Also, later we will look deeper into the writings of the prophet Daniel.

As I was finishing my research concerning Jesus' first coming, the thought occurred to me once again – "When will mankind acknowledge and accept the truth concerning Jesus Christ?" But I cannot answer for mankind, nor can I answer for you. Each of us must answer for ourselves. Please allow the Holy Spirit to help you answer once and for all, in your heart and mind, the awesome question he asked his disciples: "Who do you say that I am?"

CHAPTER 3

JESUS: THE SON OF MAN

In this chapter, I want us to take a good, long look into the earthly ministry of Jesus. We have already discussed the purpose for his first coming – the cross. He was born to die – he came to be a sacrifice for the removal of sin for all who believe (John 3:16, Romans 3:23, 623). Yet, what can we glean from studying his teaching, his methods of ministry, parables, miracles, interaction with people (particularly the twelve), and his 'example?' Was he really about love, compassion and faithfulness? What does the Bible say about these things?

Let us begin first by examining the messianic title that Jesus used most – "Son of Man". The scriptures teach very clearly that Jesus Christ was both "Son of Man" and "Son of God". He was both human and divine. The term "Son of Man" is used ninety-three times in the book of Ezekiel, each time it is applied to the humanity of the prophet as an instrument in the hand of the true and living God. The first time "son of man" is used in direct reference to Messiah is found in Daniel 7:13-14

"In my vision at night I looked, and there before me was one like a son of man, coming with the clouds of heaven. He approached the Ancient of Days and was led into His presence. He (this son of man) was given authority, glory, and sovereign power; all peoples, nations and men of every language worshipped him. His dominion is an everlasting dominion that will not pass away and his kingdom is one that will never be destroyed."

In chapters two, seven and eight the prophet Daniel interprets or personally experiences dreams and/or visions. In these visions, God reveals to Daniel that there will be four great human empires. Daniel lived at the time of the terrible Babylonian exile – the nation of Israel fell to the power of Babylon and was taken into captivity. The great Medo-Persian Empire conquered Babylon in 539 B.C. Alexander the Great conquered the Medo-Persians in 330 B.C., with the Roman Empire taking over word domination in 63 B.C. This is a quick synopsis of the four great earthly empires more on this later – setting the stage for the eschatological (end time) events. Daniel differentiates between the four kingdoms of man (all have a beginning date and an ending date) and the kingdom of the "Son of Man" – His rule will be forever throughout time and eternity! We can look back in history and see clearly that these great empires have come and gone. God's prophecy for all to see and hear IS TRUE, ACCURATE AND RELIABLE!

Daniel states in his vision of chapter seven that he saw, (V.13)

> *"... one like a son of man, coming with the clouds of heaven."*

In the four Gospels, Jesus used this title "Son of Man" 81 times to describe himself, his mission, ministry and purpose. Yet, it was never used by anyone else to describe Jesus in the same Gospel accounts. In Mark 14:62, when asked by the high priest,

> *"Are you the Christ (Greek word for Messiah), the Son of the Blessed One?"*

Jesus responded,

> *"I am and you will see the Son of Man sitting at the right hand of the Mighty One and coming on the clouds of heaven."*

In Psalm 110.1, David writes,

> *"The LORD says to my Lord: "Sit at my right hand until I make your enemies a footstool for your feet".*

In Matthew 22:44, Jesus, speaking to the Pharisees about the question,

"Whose son is the Christ?"

uses the Psalm 110:1 quote to bring two most important prophecies concerning the true identity of the "Son of Man"! David's prophecy states that Messiah will be given the seat of honor at the Mighty One's right hand. Jesus, in the Mark 14:62 verse, confirms that he is the one the Pharisees will see seated at the right hand of the Father. In the same verse, Jesus confirms Daniel's prophecy that the "Son of Man" will be coming on the clouds of heaven! The writer of Hebrews, beginning with chapter one verse 13, uses David's revelation in Psalm 110:1 as reference ten times throughout the book to point out that Jesus is Messiah the "Son of Man". What more does a Holy God have to do to reveal His True One and Only Son? The Old Testament scriptures are in perfect harmony with the New Testament scriptures – SON OF MAN = Jesus Christ!

John, writing in the book of Revelation 1:12-13 says,

> *"I turned around to see the voice that was speaking to me and when I turned I saw seven golden lampstands, and among the lampstands was someone "like a son of man", dressed in a robe reaching down to his feet and with a golden sash around his chest."*

In this passage the golden lampstands are the seven churches, as Jesus explains the mystery in verse 20. The "Son of man's" full-length robe is a direct reference to Christ's position in the "true" church as high priest, which is fully supported by the description of the golden sash about his chest. The Old Testament reference is Exodus 28:4 when the Lord God of Israel was instructing Moses as to the appropriate garments that He wanted His priests to wear.

Another important "Son of Man" reference is found in Mark 8:31. Here Jesus shares with the disciples his role as the "Suffering Servant", which fulfills the prophecy found in Isaiah 52:13 – 53:12. We will look at these two passages in depth in the next chapter as they pertain to Messiah's death, burial and resurrection.

Why Obey?

One of the most important teachings of the Christian faith is obedience. We look in 1 Samuel 15:22 where King Saul has directly disobeyed the Lord by taking plunder from victory over the Amalekites. Samuel, God's representative, has to rebuke and correct the king by speaking truth –

> *"Does the Lord delight in burnt offerings and sacrifices as much as in obeying the voice of the Lord? To obey is better than sacrifice and to heed is better than the fat of rams."*

God reveals His heart concerning His desire for His children. Therefore, the Messiah/Son of Man must live out or demonstrate obedience to the God he represents. In John 6:38 Jesus makes his overall mission goal very clear by saying,

> *"For I have come down from heaven, not to do*
> *my will but to do the will of Him who sent me."*

Here, he states the purpose of his coming is to accomplish his Father's purpose. As far as "coming down from heaven" – John 3:13 sheds even more light,

> *"No one has ever gone into heaven except the*
> *one who came from heaven - the Son of Man."*

The Savior had to be perfect in his obedience to the one who sent him. In John 4:34 Jesus says

> *"My food is to do the will of Him who sent me*
> *and to finish His work."*

According to the major theme in John's Gospel, Jesus achieved this through his life of love (agape) and sacrifice – his obedience even unto death – and was honored by the Father as shown by his resurrection.

Another example of Jesus' obedience was demonstrated at his baptism. In Matthew 3:13-17, "Then Jesus came from Galilee to the Jordan to be baptized by John. But John tried to deter him, saying

> *"I need to be baptized by you, and do you come to me?" Jesus replied, "Let it be so now; it is proper for us to do this to fulfill all righteousness. Then John consented. As soon as Jesus was baptized, he went up out of the water. At that moment heaven was opened, and he saw the Spirit of God descending like a dove and lighting on him. And a voice from heaven said, "This is my Son, whom I love, with him I am well pleased."*

Jesus' Public Ministry

Jesus' baptism marked the opening or beginning of his public Messianic ministry. John attempted to stop Jesus from coming to him for baptism, knowing Jesus had no sin from which to repent. Yet, John knew the scriptures and had been filled with the Holy Spirit from birth (Luke 1:15). Therefore, when Jesus said, "Let it be so now", John obeyed – thus filling Isaiah's prophecy: (Isaiah 42:1):

> *"Here is my servant, whom I uphold, my chosen one in whom I delight; I will put my*

*Spirit on him and he will bring justice to the
nations."*

Again, obedience is very near and dear to the heart of God.

In verses sixteen and seventeen, we read that as Jesus comes up out of the water, heaven was opened. He sees the Holy Spirit descending like a dove and lights on him. The Spirit came upon the Son not to forgive his sin, but to equip him for his ministry as "Son of Man" – "Son of God" – Messiah. A voice from heaven then speaks,

*"This is my Son whom I love; with him I am
well pleased."*

Here, the Father authenticates Jesus as SON and fulfills prophecy found in Psalm 2:7,

*"I will proclaim the decree of the Lord: He
said unto me, "You are my Son, today I have
become your Father."*

Jesus' obedience in baptism also produces the New Testament's first teaching concerning the Trinity. The word *trinity* is not found in the original writings (Greek/Hebrew languages). However, the precept or principle of God the Father – God the Son – God the Holy Spirit is taught throughout scripture.

What Did Jesus' Baptism Accomplish?

In summary, Jesus' baptism accomplished three main purposes. One, he was approved by the Father - "in whom I am well pleased." When Jesus stated: "do this to fulfill all righteousness" – he fulfilled or completed all of the Father's righteous requirements to be Messiah. Secondly, Jesus – by allowing himself to be baptized (even though he was sinless), fully identifies himself with mankind's sin. Thus, he became our propitiation or substitution (2Corinthians 5:21). Thirdly, Jesus was not afraid to be an example for all who would follow him. he desires his people, all believers, to follow his example of obedience to the Father.

Jesus' Pattern of Ministry

While ministering publicly for three years, Jesus established a pattern for his followers. The pattern is that of servanthood. In today's culture, this concept is no more popular than any other time in history; quite frankly it is less valued than ever. Most people ask questions of others such as "How many people work for you?" or "How many people do you have under your supervision?" Really what they are saying is, "How many people do you have serving you?" Two of the disciples asked a similar question; as a matter of fact their mother came and asked Jesus herself. In Matthew 20:20-28 we find this exchange:

"Then the mother of Zebedee's sons (James & John) came to Jesus with her sons and kneeling down, asked a favor of him, "What is it you want?" he asked. She said, "Grant that one of these two sons of mine may sit at your right and the other at your left in your Kingdom." "You don't know what you are asking," Jesus said unto them "Can you drink the cup I am going to drink?" "We can," they answered. Jesus said to them, "You will indeed drink from my cup, but to sit at my right or left is not for me to grant. These places belong to those for whom they have been prepared by my Father. When the ten heard about this, they were indignant with the two brothers. Jesus called them together and said, "You know that the rulers of the Gentiles lord it over them, and their high officials exercise authority over them. Not so with you. Instead, whoever wants to become great among you must be your servant and whoever wants to be first must be your slave– just as the Son of Man did not come to be served, but to serve, and to give his life as a ransom for many."

Wow! James and John – aren't you two glad you and your Mom asked that question? As adult males, even today, to have your Mother come to ask the leader of your organization to be his top "right hand" associate – how embarrassing! Also, the other ten "disciples" find out and do not take the news particularly well. Of course, Jesus handles this potentially divisive situation with his usual strength of character (based on love-agape and truth). Look in the passage;

he doesn't scold the mother, or the sons, or the other ten for becoming indignant with James and John. Jesus teaches them by speaking the truth in love. At no time does he lose his emotional composure by arbitrarily lashing out at anyone. Jesus recognizes that they are all on the same team - the Father's Team.

Self-Will or God's Will?

The request itself seems to be selfish, because it *is* selfish. We must understand that "self will" is the number one chief competitor to God's will in our lives. Jesus does not criticize – he gently corrects by pointing out,

> *"You don't know what you are asking, Can you*
> *drink the cup I am going to drink?"*

We today are just like James and John – we are born with a sin nature or a self-seeking mentality. Our God sees our lives in the awesome light of eternity; we see or make requests based on our little, limited experience. These two did not understand that Jesus' cup contained the wrath of God poured out on him. He took all of mankind's sin upon himself on the cross! No other person can ever truthfully make that claim. When this request came to the other ten disciples' attention, Jesus knew action was needed – Satan was attempting to divide and conquer. In John 10:10, Jesus teaches us about Satan and his attacks on believers,

> *"The thief comes only to steal, kill and destroy; I have come that they may have life, and have it to the full."*

In Psalm 65:11 the psalmist writes,

> *"You crown the year with your bounty, and your carts will overflow with abundance."*

In a nutshell, *Jesus reveals to us that* God wants to bless His people. However, to receive God's best for our lives, we must be willing to live our lives His way! His way involves being willing to be a servant to all. In Matthew 20:25 Jesus reminds the group that his followers are to be different from the world's leaders. True believers are not to lord their position of authority over others but be willing to be their servant. Churches that are truly growing spiritually today are those who have a grasp on this truth of servanthood. These local church bodies have pastors, staff, elders, deacons, teachers and leaders who are willing to humbly serve others and in so doing serve the Lord of Lords and King of Kings. God always rewards those who humbly serve Him and who humbly serve others.

Jesus' Style: Teachings, Miracles, Parables

One of the most profound teachings of Jesus is found in the Gospel of John chapter fifteen. This instruction serves as a vivid reminder of his union with the Father and a union each believer has in Jesus. At the time Jesus shared this information with the disciples, they had just shared the Passover Feast. He was preparing them for the time when he would leave them. The "cross" loomed ahead, betrayal was to take place, the "flock" would be scattered, for the Good Shepherd was about to be struck - thus fulfilling the prophetic voice of Zechariah 13:7,

> *"Strike the shepherd, and the sheep will be scattered'.*

Jesus echoed this part of the verse in Matthew 26:31. Now Christ speaks in John 15:1-5:

> *"I am the true vine, and my Father is the gardener. He cuts off every branch in me that bears no fruit, while every branch that does bear fruit he prunes so that it will be even more fruitful. You are already clean because of the word I have spoken to you. Remain in*

*me, and I will remain in you. No branch can
bear fruit by itself; it must remain in the vine.
Neither can you bear fruit unless you remain
in me. I am the vine, you are the branches. If a
man remains in me and I in him, he will bear
much fruit; apart from me you can do
nothing."*

Here Jesus was teaching spiritual truths while using an example with which most everyone could identify. He is the true vine – or true way to the Father and heaven. In John 14:6, Jesus says,

*"I am the way and the truth and the life. No
one comes to the Father except through me."*

In this 21st century day in which we live, one of political correctness, all-inclusive language and hate speech, his words speak louder and clearer than ever. God does not exclude anyone – Acts 2:21, "All who call upon the name of the Lord shall be saved." Jesus is simply showing mankind the Way. In this teaching from the vine, He is outlining for believers some simple yet profound truths concerning our intimate and personal relationship with Him.

Jesus is the Vine

Jesus is the vine – God the Father is the gardener. If you have ever had a garden - flowers or vegetables or known someone who has, you know of the wonderful, gentle and tender care often given by that earthly gardener. Those plants need water, sunlight, fertilizer, protection from weeds and insects and space to grow. Most of the time these tasks were the responsibility of the gardener. Our heavenly Father is the perfect Gardener. He tends to the garden of our hearts. It's the most important garden in the universe to Him.

Bruce Wilkinson, in his book, "The Secrets of the Vine" points out the Greek word for "cut off" in verse two is *airo*. First, a clearer translation of the Greek word airo, rendered in John 15 as "take away", would be "take up" or "lift up". In fact, in both the Bible and in Greek literature, airo never means "cut off". Wilkinson goes on to point out that airo interpreted as "cut off" or "remove" is not a clear translation. In this picture in verse two now we see clearly that our heavenly Father "lifts us up" in our time of need. Why? Because He wants our lives to be even more fruitful, even more blessed. In verse three, believers are already clean or forgiven because of our choice to receive the Word of Salvation from Jesus. He encourages us to remain in him, moment by moment and breath by breath. We cannot produce the fruit God desires unless we are firmly committed to Jesus. True, God loves us right where we are – but a greater truth yet, is that he loves us so much he will not leave us where we are! He desires for us to grow closer and closer to him and into deeper, more intimate personal fellowship with him. We cannot have an ever-growing closer walk with God without remaining in or staying extremely close to Jesus. He is the Vine – we (believers) are the branches. Christ Himself promises that if we remain in him – he will remain in us and produce an abundance of fruit in our lives. He even gives us a loving warning,

...“apart from me you can do nothing.”

As if he were a most helpful guide leading us through a most dangerous place (for which I think this world qualifies). He encourages us to stay close to him! There are awesome promises found in John fifteen – the promises of ever-increasing fruitfulness, the coming of the Holy Spirit, becoming God's friends – all and more are ours when we choose to remain in His love.

God's Love Produces Miracles

God's love also produces miracles. The writer of Hebrews points out (Chapter 2:3-4),

> *“...This salvation which was first announced by the Lord, was confirmed to us by those who heard him. God also testified to it by signs, wonders and various miracles and gifts of the Holy Spirit distributed according to his will.”*

The message of salvation through Christ Jesus was confirmed to the first century church by many eyewitnesses of Jesus, as well as the demonstration of his power that produced miracles, signs and wonders. His first miracle was changing the water into wine at the wedding feast found in John chapter two. This miracle was more about relationship than something to drink, for in the first century, a wedding celebration with no wine to drink would have been a major embarrassment for the host family. Most of Jesus' miracles include: healings of leprosy, blindness, freedom from demon-possession, curing deafness and the inability to speak, and healing the woman with the blood disorder; all demonstrating his power over sickness and disease. Jesus also demonstrated his power over nature by calming the storm, walking on water, the feedings of the five thousand and four thousand respectively, cursing of the fig tree and the large catches of fish.

The Power of the Lord

Our Lord also demonstrated his power over death by three separate incidences of raising people from the dead. First, Jairus' daughter, then the widow's son at Nain and lastly, Mary's and Martha's brother, a man by the name of Lazarus. I would like for us to take a close look into the biblical account of the first time Lazarus died.

This story is found in the eleventh chapter of John's Gospel. Beginning in verse three, the sisters sends word to Jesus that Lazarus is sick. He responds,

"This sickness will not end in death. No, it is for God's glory so that God's Son may be glorified through it".

Jesus loved this family, yet he does something that seems strange to most. He does not rush to the scene, as a matter of fact, he stays put for two more days. Then he announces to the disciples that it's time to "go back to Judea." This causes great concern from the twelve as the Jews in Judea recently attempted to stone Jesus. He reassures them that this is exactly what needs to be done. As Jesus arrives, he discovers "that Lazarus has been in the tomb for four days". There is still a great crowd gathered to mourn with the family. Jewish tradition provided for three days of extremely heavy mourning, four days of heavy mourning followed by lighter mourning for thirty days; thus the large crowd of people.

When Martha, sister of Lazarus, heard that Jesus was coming, she went out to meet him. "*Lord,* Martha said to Jesus, *if you had been here my brother would not have died.* But I know that even God will give you whatever you ask." What awesome yet simple child-like faith! Martha has spent enough time with Messiah to recognize his close relationship to the Father. Jesus responds, "*Your brother will rise again.*" Martha answers,

"I know he will rise again in the resurrection at the last day." Jesus says, "I am the resurrection and the life. He who believes in

44

me will live even though he dies; and whoever lives and believes in me will never die. Do you believe this"? "Yes, Lord", she exclaims, "I believe that you are the true Christ, the Son of God, who was to come into the world."

This is the purpose of Lazarus death. This is why Jesus tarried for two more days before leaving and walking on the two-day journey to arrive at the place where the family lived. His perfect timing! Jesus allowed Lazarus to die as he stated earlier, to Glorify God by having the eyewitnesses of this miraculous event to believe in Jesus as Messiah – Son of the Most High God! One can only imagine how many souls have come to faith in Christ by the preaching or sharing of this amazing story of God's power over death! John, the writer of this Gospel confirms his purpose in writing his account of Jesus life and ministry in John 20:30-31,

"Jesus did many other miraculous signs in the presence of his disciples, which are not recorded in this book. But these are written that you may believe that Jesus is the Christ, the Son of God, and that by believing you may have life in his name".

In His economy, God continues today to use any and every means to reveal Jesus Christ as Savior of the world! Now let's go back to the tomb of Lazarus.

Jesus Breaks Up a Funeral

He has arrived fully knowing what the scene will be – crying, weeping, mourning, questions, regrets – if only … Yet, as he views this sight of Mary, who has now come out to greet him, weeping Jesus

> *"was deeply moved in spirit and troubled. "Where have you laid him?" he asked. They reply, "Come and see, Lord." Jesus wept. Then the Jews said, "See how he loved him!" But some of them said, "Could not he who opened the eyes of the blind man have kept this man from dying?"*

Many of us, in our scripture memorization, have recognized the shortest verse in the Bible – "Jesus wept". Yet, we often skim right over the significance of this awesome truth – our God is deeply touched by our pain and suffering. Our God chose to step out of heaven and into a human body that not only hurts when it is bruised but also experiences the emotional and psychological sides of the human condition. The writer of Hebrews puts it best in chapter four verse fifteen,

"For we do not have a high priest who is unable to sympathize with our weaknesses, but we have one who has been tempted in every way, just as we are – yet was without sin."

I strongly dislike a popular phrase of our generation – "I feel your pain". My immediate response is "No you do not!" The truth of the matter is Jesus is the only one who does feel and has felt our pain, the excruciating pain of our sin.

In the midst of all the pain and anguish that he was experiencing, the Son of God stayed focused on his mission. After

"being deeply moved once more, Jesus comes to the tomb. "Take the stone away", he said. "But Lord", said Martha, sister of the dead man, "by this time there is a bad odor, for he has been there four days."

Is not that response just like our human nature? God is about to do something wonderful and we bog down in the logical facts. We bog down in our experience, our knowledge, our ability to understand through our sensory perception. Yet, God continues to challenge and encourage us to respond to Him by faith. Hebrews 11:6 reminds us:

"And without faith it is impossible to please God, because anyone who comes to Him must believe that He exists and that He rewards those who earnestly seek Him." Jeremiah 29:13 adds, "You will seek me and find me when you seek me with all your heart."

Faith - believing in him even when it is outside of our knowledge, experience or ability to comprehend. When you think about this truth, many things are outside of our ability to understand them, yet we take them on face value and believe. For example, computers, technology, modern medicine, astrophysics, etc. - You do not need to fully understand a gasoline combustible engine to use a car for transportation – the most important thing you hope for is the car starts when you turn the key. There it is, the key to learning and discovering more about God – His ways and purposes – His plan, hopes and dreams for your life is FAITH!

Jesus responds to Martha's stating the facts by saying,

"Did I not tell you that if you believed, you would see the glory of God?"

As they took the stone away, Jesus looks up and offers this brief yet powerful prayer,

"Father, I thank you that you have heard me. I know that you always hear me, but I said this

for the benefit of the people standing here that
they may believe that you sent me."

Everything God does has a purpose; He wastes nothing. He has allowed things to take place in your life for a reason, a higher purpose – to draw you into an intimate, personal relationship with Himself – that you may believe that God the Father sent God the Son to make it all possible.

After his prayer,

> *"Jesus called in a loud voice, "Lazarus come out!" The dead man came out, his hands and feet wrapped with strips of linen and a cloth around his face. Jesus said to them, "Take off the grave clothes and let him go."*

Based on this awesome truth of Jesus' miraculous power over death, I am compelled to ask you a very personal question. **What is in your life today that needs to be raised from the dead?** A relationship, a commitment, a promise you have broken to God, yourself or a loved one? Do you need more love, joy, peace, grace, mercy, blessing, or hope? I, like Jeremiah, want to encourage you – right where you are, to "seek Him with all your heart" for then is when you will find Him. And in finding Christ, all the blessings of God will be yours. Take a moment right now and ask Jesus to come into your life today. He is the only one who can raise us from the dead!

The Parables of Jesus

As we look into Jesus' teachings we cannot help but see the many parables he used to teach his followers. The word *parable* in the Greek simply means "a placing beside". In our language a parable could be called an illustration or comparison. "We find no parables in the Gospel of John as he focused on Jesus' many figures of speech. However, in the synoptic Gospels – Matthew, Mark and Luke we find about thirty different stories that Jesus drew from nature and everyday human life experiences."[2] There are parables concerning lost sheep, a mustard seed, tenants, one about ten virgins, talents (a unit of money), comparison of sheep and goats, one about a wayward son and other topics with which Jesus' audience could relate. Yet, there is one that I believe stands at the center of his teaching – the parable of the sower.

The Parable of the Sower

We find this particular parable in the thirteenth chapter of Matthew's Gospel. This teaching is also found in Mark's and Luke's Gospels. In this illustration of the sower, Jesus explains or interprets its true meaning. He seldom did this. In Matthew 12:10 the disciples ask,

"Why do you speak to the people in parables?"
Jesus responds, "The knowledge of the secrets
of the kingdom of heaven has been given to
you, but not to them."

The term "secrets of the kingdom of heaven" does not imply or teach that God is withholding any information from these people. The fact of the matter is that the disciples had already received the "secret" that God is fulfilling His promised Kingdom through the coming of His Son. The disciples, just like you, me and everyone else, had to respond to Jesus by faith. When he called each one to "come follow me" they did so by faith. Thus, Jesus taught the "spiritually dull" by illustrations – things that everyone could relate to in order that they would believe. Yet the cold, hard reality was that the people's hearts had grown calloused. Jesus further explains beginning in verse thirteen,

"This is why I speak to them in parables:
Through seeing, they do not see; through
hearing, they do not hear or understand. In
them is fulfilled the prophecy of Isaiah: You
will be ever hearing but never understanding;
you will be ever seeing but never perceiving.
For this people's heart has become calloused;
they hardly hear with their ears and they have
closed their eyes. Otherwise, they might see

with their eyes, hear with their ears,
understand with their hearts and turn, and I
would heal them."

More Fulfilled Prophecy

Not only did Jesus fulfill Isaiah's prophecy, he also fulfilled what the Psalmist wrote concerning Messiah in Psalm 78:2 (and Matthew 13:35) – it reads:

> *"I will open my mouth in parables, I will utter*
> *hidden things, things from of old."*

Meaning that Jesus the Great Teacher, Prophet, Messiah will come teaching truth that was hidden since the creation of the world. We do not need misapplication here – the truth was hidden because of man's sin NOT because God was hiding anything from us, for we are His children created in His image. God desires to heal all people – that healing comes by believing in God's one and only Son. Also, at this point in Jesus' earthly ministry it was not time to reveal the whole truth concerning his Messiah-ship. There was still much to do in the way of teaching, miracles, discipling the twelve and fulfilling prophecy before he would be ready to go to the cross – the ultimate fulfillment of his first coming.

Upon further review, let's examine what Jesus intended for the listener to learn. In Matthew 13:18, Jesus speaks,

"Listen then to what the parable of the sower means: When anyone hears the message about the kingdom and does not understand it, the evil one comes and snatches away what was sown in his heart. This is the seed sown along the path. The one who received the seed that fell on rocky places is the man who hears the word and at once receives it with joy. But since he has no root, he lasts only a short time. When trouble or persecution comes because of the word, he quickly falls away. The one who received the seed that fell among the thorns is the man who hears the word, but the worries of this life and the deceitfulness of wealth choke it, making it unfruitful. But the one who received the seed that fell on good soil is the man who hears the word and understands it. He produces a crop yielding a hundred, sixty or thirty times what was sown."

Our Lord could not have been any clearer. The first example, "the seed that fell along the path", teaches us that we are in a spiritual battle. As a pastor, I have seen this many times, a person hears the Gospel message and just does not understand it. Jesus points out that the evil one (Satan) is responsible for snatching the seed away from that person in an effort to keep that individual in darkness! We need to continue our all-out prayer effort for all of those people – precious to the Father – who are still walking around in darkness; those who have no spiritual understanding or discernment as to who Jesus Christ really is. We will win this fight "on our knees."

The second seed sown has its own revelations. The "seed that fell on rocky places" is the person who hears the word and immediately receives it with joy. Sadly, I witness this too often as well. An individual comes to a worship service, hears the "good news", gets all excited as if this truth is exactly what they have been searching and longing for. Yet, as they attempt to share this new truth, rejection comes – "Trouble or persecution comes because of the Word", they quickly shrink back or tragically fall away. In Lukc 14:27, Jesus instructs the large crowds who were following him around by saying,

> *"... anyone who does not carry his cross and*
> *follow me cannot be my disciple."*

This Luke passage sheds light on the parable of the sower – count the cost of following Christ. He "does not want a blind, naïve commitment that expects only blessing". [3] Jesus has paid the ultimate price for our salvation by taking our place on the cross. In this deepest of all relationships, should he not expect and receive our best? The "seed" that fell among the thorns is perhaps the most frustrating of the three types of people who choose not to follow Christ. This person also hears the Word, and understands it, but allows the worries of this life and the deceitfulness of material possessions to possess him – thus choking out God's truth. This is why Jesus taught in Luke 16:13

> *"... You cannot serve both God and money."*
> Paul teaches in 1 Timothy 6:10,

> *"For the love of money is a root of all kinds of evil. Some people, eager for money, have wandered from the faith and pierced themselves with many griefs."*

God desires His followers to be faithful stewards over all He has entrusted to them. This "seed" fails to trust in God as Provider and seeks rather to trust in the dead end street of materialism - only tragically to discover that they cannot take one stitch with them when this life is over. Our possessions, our education, our income, our careers, prestige or status – none of these can save our souls – only Jesus.

The fourth and final seed is very encouraging. This is one who "hears the Word and understands it". This person takes God at His Word – believes and receives by faith. Check out the promise that goes with this individual,

"he produces a crop, yielding a hundred, sixty
or thirty times what was sown."

The life that is yielded to Christ is one that is going to be productive. Not in the world's ways of measuring success, but where it really counts – the economy of the Creator of the Universe! He desires His people to be found faithful, not necessarily successful in the eyes of the world. Yet, His Word is clear, as He spoke to Joshua in Joshua 1:8,

> *"Do not let this Book of the Law depart from your mouth; meditate on it day and night, so that you may be careful to do everything written in it. Then you will be prosperous and successful."*

> God is very serious about His Word – He has gone to great lengths, sometimes moving heaven and earth to ensure we have an opportunity to hear His truth. Now it is up to us! – Obey? Or disobey? That truly is the question.

Summary

We have covered a fair amount of ground concerning Jesus' first earthly ministry. However, in no way have we looked at even a small portion of the truths available to the faithful student of His Word. Jesus was faithful to the Father's plan and purpose. We, as His followers, should do likewise.

CHAPTER 4

THE CROSS

When we survey the significance of the cross of Jesus Christ, it is difficult to honestly evaluate without viewing the harsh reality of death. He died on a Roman cross. This was the first century symbol of being punished to death for being a criminal. In the movie, "Passion of the Christ," Mel Gibson openly portrays the horrific torture of one who would be sentenced to die by crucifixion. The Roman mindset was to display power and might against anyone who dare break the law of the empire. The thought was that crucifixion would be so devastatingly brutal and barbaric that it would be the ultimate deterrent to crime. Yet, Jesus had broken no law; furthermore he had committed no sin. In this chapter, we will explore why the Father allowed the Son to die such an inexpressibly horrible death. We will take a further look into the crucifixion, his death and burial; the predictions and prophecies concerning his death; and the purposes and atonement of his death. Let us begin our study with a background look into the God of the cross.

Death on a Cross?

What kind of God would allow His Son to die on a pagan cross? In the book of Ezekiel, God is speaking to and through the prophet to the nation of Israel concerning the importance of refraining from deliberate sin and disobedience. God questions in Ezekiel 18:23,

> "Do I take any pleasure in the death of the
> wicked? declares the Sovereign Lord. Rather,
> am I not pleased when they turn from their
> ways and live?"

God reminds Israel and the world that He takes no pleasure in the death of a wicked person, much less His perfect sinless Son. In this eighteenth chapter of Ezekiel, God once again lays out His hope for the people - turn away from sin and live. In verses thirty-one and thirty-two, God exposes His heart for all people,

> "Rid yourself of all the offenses you have
> committed and get a new heart and a new
> spirit. Why will you die, O house of Israel? For
> I take no pleasure in the death of anyone,
> declares the Sovereign Lord. Repent and live!"

He is saying clearly and passionately: turn away from what causes death – namely our sin and disobedience – and live. Ezekiel reminds us that this is not a creed or suggestion coming from the prophet – but a call of commitment from the Creator, a declaration from the "Sovereign Lord." He promises to give the individual a new heart and new spirit when the person turns away from his or her sin. The apostle Peter echoes this truth centuries later in 2 Peter 3:9,

> *"The Lord is not slow in keeping his promise,*
> *as some understand slowness. He is patient*
> *with you not wanting anyone to perish, but*
> *everyone to come to repentance."*

The God of the Old Testament is the God of the New Testament! God's plan for salvation of the human race – a personal relationship with the Creator – did not, has not and will not change. All the way back to Moses, God desired His people (followers) to choose life. Beginning in Deuteronomy 30:11, the Lord speaks,

> *"Now what I am commanding you today is*
> *not too difficult for you or beyond your reach*
> *... No, the word is very near you; it is in your*
> *mouth and in your heart so you may obey it."*

God placed His word in the people's hearts and mouths in order to help them obey. However, we have the freedom to choose, verse fifteen,

"See, I set before you today life and prosperity, death and destruction. For I command you today to love the Lord your God, to walk in his ways, and keep his commands, decrees and laws; then you will live and increase, and the Lord your God will bless you in the land you are trying to possess."

Our heavenly Father loves us and gives us freedom to choose Him or reject Him. He is clear in His call – choose God and you receive "life and prosperity" - reject God and you receive "death and destruction." In verses nineteen and twenty, the Lord shares one more plea with His people,

"Now choose life, so that you and your children may live and that you may love the Lord your God, listen to his voice and hold fast to him. For the Lord is your life ..."

Here God is pleading with the people to choose life in a personal (love, listen, hold) intimate relationship with Him. What is holding us back from choosing life? The Psalmist – King David gives us a clue in Psalm 51:5,

"Surely I was sinful at birth, sinful from the time my mother conceived me."

David, King of Israel, realizes the depravity of the human heart, thus recognizing that human beings are born with a major problem – sin. Webster's dictionary defines sin as a natural "bent" or inclination to that which is wrong.[1] In verse seven, David asks God to,

> *"cleanse me with hyssop, and I will be clean;*
> *wash me and I will be whiter than snow."*

The term "cleanse me" in the Hebrew literally means 'un-sin me" or remove my disobedience and restore me to a right relationship with you O Lord. David knows that he cannot do this, for only God and He alone can forgive sin and restore the sinner in the right relationship to God that was intended from the beginning. This restoration or cleansing comes down from the Creator to the created. But how does that happen?

The Old Testament Foretold the Crucifixion

Let us begin with the prophecies concerning Messiah and his death. In Isaiah 52:13-15,

> *"See, my servant will act wisely (or will prosper), he will be raised and lifted up and highly exalted. Just as there were many who were appalled at him – his appearance was so disfigured beyond that of any man and his form marred beyond human likeness – so will*

he sprinkle many nations, and kings will shut
their mouths because of him. For what they
were not told they will see and what they have
not heard, they will understand."

In today's modern world, there are many countries where it is against the law to share the Gospel – Muslim nations like Iran, Afghanistan, Saudi Arabia, and Indonesia; Hindu countries like India. Communist China is another; yet God is the God of the Impossible! He will get His Good News in these lands – to these people – some will reject – others will accept – for *they will understand.*

In verse thirteen, God is speaking about his representative – Messiah, which he will lead wisely and will prosper. This prosperity includes Israel and all the nations of the earth. Yet, before this "age" of prosperity, Messiah must suffer by paying the price or "ransom" for humanity's sin. Look at the phrase "he will be raised and lifted up and highly exalted". Jesus said in John 12:32,

"But I, when I am lifted up from the earth, will
draw all men to Myself."

Jesus – Messiah had to go to the cross. Before, Jesus is highly exalted he must suffer. This is Isaiah's message to the nation of Israel that when they see One coming in the name of the Lord, one who fulfills all prophecy and completes the Fathers requirement by going to the cross – Here is your Savior! I have often wondered how those religious leaders in the first century could miss their Savior. Well, it's the same way people of the twenty-first century miss him – they choose to reject his sacrifice on the cross. In Isaiah 52:14 it says,

> *"... many who were appalled at him – his appearance was so disfigured ... and his form marred beyond human likeness"* – our sin is the cause for such disfiguring, marring and suffering! Thus, confirming,

"God so loved the world!" Look in verse fifteen, "*...kings will shut their mouths because of him.*" Even though these kings "were not told" of the prophecies – when they hear and receive the Gospel they will see! Even though these kings, "have not heard" of the prophecies – they will understand his mission when they see his suffering and coming exaltation. This question is often raised, "How could a loving God allow His Son to suffer so?" The answer is simple, "There is NO OTHER WAY!" Paul confirms this truth in Romans 5:8,

> *"God demonstrates His own love for us in this: While we were still sinners, Christ died for us."*

Suffering Comes First

The suffering must come first, then the exaltation – it is God's way. Isaiah 49:6b-7,

"I will also make you a light for the Gentiles, that you may bring My salvation to the ends of the earth. This is what the Lord says – the Redeemer and Holy One of Israel – to him who was despised and abhorred by the nation, to the servant of rulers: Kings will see you and rise up, princes will see and bow down, because of the Lord, who is faithful, the Holy One of Israel, who has chosen you."

In this passage, we clearly see a synopsis of God's plan of salvation. The Father is speaking to the Messiah –

"I will also make you a light for the Gentiles that you may bring my salvation to the ends of the earth."

God's plan for Israel and the nations is clear – everyone can have a relationship with God and that relationship is made possible through the "cross".

Looking further, in Isaiah, chapter fifty three – the passage of scripture that details the awesome suffering of Messiah -- Verse one,

"Who has believed our message and to whom has the arm of the Lord been revealed?"

This is more than poetic license – the prophet is going to answer this question of "who has believed our message" by revealing the truth about the suffering servant. "Who?" is answered by all who put their faith in the sacrificial death of Christ Jesus. In John 12:38, Jesus quotes this verse when applying the question of "who" to the Jews rejection of him as Messiah. In Psalm 98:2-3,

> *"The Lord has made his salvation known and revealed his righteousness to the nations. He has remembered his love and his faithfulness to the house of Israel; all the ends of the earth have seen the salvation of our God."*

The Creator has gone to great lengths to reveal His salvation to both Israel and the nations.

Isaiah fifty-three, verse two says,

> *"He grew up before him like a tender shoot, and like a root out of dry ground. He had no beauty or majesty to attract us to him, nothing in his appearance that we should desire him."*

This was totally God's plan. Jesus had humble beginnings in a manger, not a castle. He was born to a young virgin, not to an earthly king or queen. He was raised in lowly surroundings in Nazareth, not in the king's palace. There was nothing of his appearance that would attract us to him. What a beautiful plan – for when we examine these items that stem from verse two – all of them would (or at least could) lead someone to follow Jesus for all the wrong reasons. God looks at the heart, He desires His followers to "worship Him in spirit and in truth."

Isaiah fifty three, verse three,

> "He was despised and rejected by men, a man
> of sorrows and familiar with suffering. Like
> one from whom men hide their faces He was
> despised, and we esteemed him not."

The psalmist illustrates this when he writes in Psalm 69:4,

> "Those who hate me without reason
> outnumber the hairs of my head; many are my
> enemies without cause, those who seek to
> destroy me."

Jesus, in John 15:25, refers to this passage as a fulfillment of prophecy when he stated,

> "But this is to fulfill what is written in their
> law: They hated me without reason."

It is no different today than when that first century mob cried out, "Crucify him!" Who would believe that in twenty-first century

America – a land founded on Judeo-Christian principles – people would be asked not to close public prayers in Jesus' name. There is truly something about that Name. In truth, a day is coming when everyone of every age will acknowledge his greatness. As Paul writes in Philippians 2:9-11,

> *"Therefore God exalted him to the highest place and gave him the name that is above every name, that at the name of Jesus every knee should bow, in heaven and on earth, and every tongue confess that Jesus Christ is Lord, to the glory of God the Father."*

The awesome prophecy in Isaiah 53:4-12 continues to reveal many of the, "little known," truths about God's plan of salvation for Israel and the nations. This saving grace comes only through Jesus Christ! I encourage you to read and study this passage as the Truth will become clearly evident.

Even as the Old Testament prophets foretold of the Suffering Servant's death, Jesus himself instructed the disciples of his coming appointment with a Roman cross. In Matthew 20:18-19, Jesus speaks,

> *"We are going up to Jerusalem, and the Son of Man will be betrayed to the chief priests and the teachers of the law. They will condemn*

him to death and will turn him over to the Gentiles to be mocked and flogged and crucified. On the third day he will be raised to life!"

Two thousand years later, we see that this is exactly what took place.

Mocked and Flogged

Jesus was mocked by the very ones he came to save. The scene starts out with the mocking of the Roman soldiers in Matthew 27:27-31,

> *"... then the governor's soldiers took Jesus into the Praetorium and gathered thc whole company of soldiers around him and then twisted together a crown of thorns and set it on his head. They put a staff in his right hand and knelt in front of him and mocked Him. 'Hail, King of the Jews!' they said. They spit on him, and took the staff and struck him on the head again and again. After they had mocked him, they took off the robe and put his own clothes on him. Then they led him away to crucify him."*

Please keep in mind that the mocking commenced after the flogging! After being almost beaten to death, the Savior endured this ridicule from not only so called "pagans" but also his own people. After the soldiers nailed him to the tree, Matthew testifies (Matthew 27:39-43,

> *"Those who passed by hurled insults at him, shaking their heads and saying, 'You who are going to destroy the temple and build it in three days save yourself! Come down from the cross, if you are the Son of God!' In the same way the chief priests, the teachers of the law and the elders mocked him, 'He saved others,' they said, 'but he can't save himself. He's the King of Israel! Let him come down now from the cross and we will believe in him. He trusts in God. Let God rescue him now if he wants him, for he said, 'I am the Son of God.'"*

Mankind's sinful nature is no different today than it was then. Many today think nothing of using Jesus' name as a curse word. Others still blame God for most of the things that are wrong in our world. These so-called "religious" people would not allow this Messiah to fit in to their picture and idea of who God really is. Jesus just did not fit their image of Savior God.

What these "religious" people failed to realize
is that their mocking lines up perfectly with
the mocking questions of Satan in Luke 4:1-9.

In this passage, known as the "Temptation of Christ," Satan attacks Jesus with the same mockery – *"If you are the Son of God..."* Each time Satan attacked Christ, Jesus sets the most excellent example by using God's Word! The most powerful weapon against evil in the universe is the Word of God! In this passage Jesus teaches his true followers to do the same. When the enemy attacks, do not argue, fret nor debate! Simply speak the Truth from God's Word! The victory is already ours – all we need to do is walk in faith and obey His Word!

Facets of the Crucifixion

There are obviously many facets of the "crucifixion" of Christ. I would like to look at just a few that come to mind. In Matthew 27:45,

"From the sixth hour until the ninth hour
darkness came over all the land."

The brightest time of day, from noon until three o'clock p.m. – it was "dark over all the land." This fulfilled Amos' prophecy (Amos 8:9),

"In that day, declares the Sovereign Lord, "I
will make the sun go down at noon and
darken the earth in broad daylight."

The Word is true – the Word is clear – still people refuse to believe. God has sent us the prophets, writers, teachers, preachers – even His Son! As Paul states in Romans 2:20, God has revealed himself clearly, even through nature – "darkness from noon until three" –

"so that men are without excuse."

Another interesting detail is at the very moment of Jesus' death, the curtain of the temple was torn in two from top to bottom (Matthew 27:51). This curtain was the inner curtain that separated the Holy Place from the Most Holy Place. The tearing of the curtain signifies Christ's making it possible for believers to go directly into God's presence ([1]NIV Study Note). An earthquake accompanied this tearing of the curtain. Matthew goes on to report that

> *"... tombs broke open and the bodies of many holy people who had died were raised to life. They came out of the tombs, and after Jesus' resurrection they went into the holy city and appeared to many people." (Matthew 27:52-53).*

We have documented in an earlier chapter Jesus' authority over nature, so this miracle should not take us by surprise.

As for physical pain and suffering, none of the Gospel writers dwell on the horrors that befell Christ. Yet we see God fulfilling His prophecies within each individual aspect of the crucifixion. The dividing of his clothing in John 19:24 fulfills Psalm 22:18. The piercing of his side in John 19:33-34, evidence that proves he truly died – not just passed out as some have erroneously claimed. John summarizes in John 19:36-37,

> *"These things happened so that scripture would be fulfilled: Not one of his bones will be broken (Exodus 12:46, Numbers 9:12, Psalm 34:20).*

Scripture also says

> *"they will look on the one they pierced"* (Zechariah 12:10).

Yes – Messiah – Jesus Christ – Suffering Servant – our ultimate Passover Lamb. Peter speaking in Acts 2:36,

> *"Therefore let all Israel be assured of this: God has made this Jesus, whom you crucified, both Lord and Christ."*

The Cross of Purpose

We start with the obvious purpose of victory over death. Believers in Jesus Christ do not ever have to fear death again. Isaiah 25:8 states,

"...He will swallow up death forever. The Sovereign Lord will wipe away the tears from all faces; He will remove the disgrace of His people from all the earth. The Lord has spoken."

Sin and death were defeated at the cross – once and for all. In first Corinthians 15:54, Paul confirms this passage,

"When the perishable has been clothed with the imperishable, and the mortal with immortality, then the saying that is written will come true: Death has been swallowed up in victory."

Isaiah's prophecy was seven hundred years before the coming of Messiah; Paul's teaching concerns the believers resurrected body, which when consummated by God will fulfill Jesus' work of redemption on the cross.

Along this same theme, Paul writes to Timothy in 2 Timothy 1:9-10,

"This grace was given us in Christ Jesus before the beginning of time, but it has now been revealed through the appearing of our Savior, Christ Jesus, who has destroyed death and has

brought life and immortality to light through
the Gospel",

Victory Over Death

This theme of "victory over death" is continued by the writer of the book of Hebrews. The writer is communicating with Jewish Christians. In chapter two, verses fourteen and fifteen, he confirms,

> *"Since the children have flesh and blood, he too shared in their humanity so that by his death he might destroy him who holds the power of death – that is, the devil – and free those who all their lives were held in slavery by their fear of death".*

Satan does not have the final authority over death, yet he tempts and causes humans to sin, thus coming under the penalty of sin, which is death. Jesus left his throne in heaven to become a man of flesh and bone that he might free all believers from sin's death sentence.

> *"Whom the Son sets free, is free indeed" (John 8:36).*

Jesus speaks a most reassuring truth in Revelation 1:18,

*"I am the Living One; I was dead and behold I
am alive for ever and ever! And I hold the keys
of death and Hades."*

Jesus has authority over all things, even death and hell. As believers, we can experience victory in this life and look forward to spending eternity living in the presence of Almighty God – death and hell have been defeated for us by Christ's sacrifice on the cross.

How to Avoid the Second Death

Hell has been labeled in the Bible as the "second death." This is where those who have rejected Jesus Christ spend their eternity and receive their punishment for their sin, namely rejection of God's wonderful plan of salvation. In Revelation 20:6, John writes this truth,

*"Blessed and holy are those who have part in
the first resurrection. The second death has no
power over them, but they will be priests of
God and of Christ and will reign with him for a
thousand years."*

We will explore this awesome promise in a later chapter. John continues in verse fourteen, *"Then death and Hades were thrown in the lake of fire. The lake of fire is the second death."* Very strong language – it has a definite sense of finality. Listen further to the words of John, speaking of God, in Revelation 21:4,

> "He will wipe every tear from their eyes. There will be no more death or mourning or crying or pain, for the old order of things has passed away."

Contrast this wonderfully bright future with that of those who refuse to receive the "power of the cross."

Amazing Atonement

In summary, Christ's death on the cross should be viewed as "atonement." The word atonement basically means reconciliation, or to "make everything right between two parties." The two parties are God and man. His perfection demanded righteousness on our part – His grace sent Jesus to perform the divine act of reconciliation – bringing all who would believe into a right relationship with Him. Paul writes in Romans 5:6,

> "You see, at just the right time, when we were still powerless, Christ died for the ungodly." In 2 Corinthians 5:21, Paul explains,

> "God made Him who had no sin to be sin for us, so that in Him we might become the righteousness of God."

78

What an awesome God we serve!

CHAPTER 5

THE RESURRECTION AND ASCENSION

OF JESUS CHRIST

Have you ever felt hopeless? Had a bad stretch of your life where seemingly everything you did turned out wrong? Ever feel like you are cursed? Had the feeling of being the wrong person, at the wrong place, at the wrong time? I have experienced that sense of hopelessness many times. I want to encourage you that even Jesus was known as a "man of sorrows." Let's examine together why we still have hope for our future (Jeremiah 29:11).

I have often shared with the congregations I have served this important truth: "Without Christmas there would be no Easter, yet without Easter – there would be no Christmas." More precisely, without the resurrection of Jesus Christ, life would be totally meaningless. As Solomon said in Ecclesiastes 1:2,

"Meaningless! Meaningless! Says the Teacher. Utterly meaningless! Everything is meaningless!"

The context here is that unless the individual's life is rightly related to God, that person's life is in vain. Paul writes in Romans 8:20-21,

"For the creation was subjected to frustration, not by its own choice, but by the will of the one who subjected it, in hope that the creation itself will be liberated from its bondage to decay and brought into the glorious freedom of the children of God."

Paul is speaking of the "curse" brought on creation by the fall of Adam and Eve as found in Genesis 3:16-19. The universe – all of creation – was never intended by our Creator to be in bondage or under the curse of sin. Through the resurrection power of Christ, man and all of creation are now destined for renewal, NOT destruction. Peter, speaking of the coming "day of the Lord," says in 2 Peter 3:13,

"But in keeping with his promise we are looking forward to a new heaven and a new earth, the home of righteousness."

John confirms this truth in Revelation, chapter twenty-one. God chooses to *"make everything new"* (Revelation 21:5). Let's explore the power behind this awesome, wonderful renewal.

Resurrection and Renewal

Isaiah predicted Messiah's resurrection, as we have already discussed in Isaiah 53:11. Jesus predicted his death and resurrection in Matthew 17: 22-23,

> *"When they came together in Galilee, He said to them, 'The Son of Man is going to be betrayed into the hands of men. They will kill Him, and on the third day He will be raised to life.'"*

The Gospel accounts of Jesus' resurrection confirm both Isaiah's and Christ's predictions. In Matthew 28:1-7 we read,

> *"After the Sabbath, at dawn on the first day of the week, Mary Magdalene and the other Mary went to look at the tomb. There was a violent earthquake, for an angel of the Lord came down from heaven and, going to the tomb, rolled back the stone and sat on it. His appearance was like lightening, and his clothes were white as snow. The guards were*

so afraid of him that they shook and became like dead men. The angel said to the women, 'Do not be afraid, for I know that you are looking for Jesus, who was crucified. He is not here; He has risen, just as He said. Come and see the place where He lay. Then go quickly and tell the disciples; "He has risen from the dead and is going ahead of you into Galilee. There you will see Him. Now, I have told you."

Mark 16:6-7 affirms this truth.

We Can Trust God and His Word

We can always trust God to confirm, affirm and uphold His Word. In both accounts, the angel reminds those at the tomb and all believers that the "resurrection" was just as Jesus had said. What a comfort – we can take our God at His Word! He has gone to such great lengths in order to have an intimate, personal relationship with all who believe. The angel even instructs these ladies to go tell all the disciples – even Peter. See, Peter needed to be forgiven and restored to right fellowship with Jesus. God already had that covered as the angel reminds them to include Peter. Our Lord is not an "exclusive" Being – He is a most gracious and "inclusive" Creator. "Whosoever will believe" is included in the family of God! Jesus speaks to this truth in John 5:24-29,

"I tell you the truth; whoever hears my word and believes Him who sent me has eternal life and will not be condemned; He has crossed over from death to life. I tell you the truth, a time is coming and has now come when the dead will hear the voice of the Son of God and those who hear the voice will live... Do not be amazed at this time, for a time is coming when all who are in their graves will hear his voice and come out."

Jesus is very clear in this passage – the plan for eternal life is, "believing in the One who has sent me." These individuals will not be condemned for they have "crossed over from death to life." ***Interesting choice of the word "crossed" spoken by our Lord.*** When one believes and receives Jesus' work on the cross, he or she eternally crosses over from death to life. It will be Jesus as the Judge of all humanity. He will judge both the believer and those who have done evil by the rejection of "His Word" and "the One who has sent Him".

What Christ's Resurrection Means for Believers

Jesus, in John 11:25, says,

"I am the resurrection and the life. He who believes in me will live, even though he dies;

and whoever lives and believes in me will
never die. Do you believe this?"

I now want us to explore biblical references that will hopefully shed more light on the deeper meanings of Jesus' resurrection. In Acts chapter two, Peter is addressing a large crowd of Jews after the celebration of Pentecost. This celebration is also called the "Feast of Weeks" (Deuteronomy 16:10), the "Feast of the Harvest" (Exodus 23:16) and the "day of first fruits" (Numbers 28:26). Therefore, Jerusalem was filled with Jews from "far and wide" who were present to celebrate the day of Pentecost. Peter speaks to them of Jesus in Acts 2:23-24,

> *"This man was handed over to you by God's set*
> *purpose and foreknowledge; and you, with the*
> *help of wicked men, put Him to death by*
> *nailing Him to the cross. But God raised Him*
> *from the dead, freeing Him from the agony of*
> *death, because it was impossible for death to*
> *keep its hold on Him."*

God's perfect timing was to send His Holy Spirit on the day of "first fruits." Do not miss this significance in Acts. For the Holy Spirit to come, Jesus had to die for the atonement of sin and be raised to life as a symbol of being our "first fruit." By God raising the Messiah from the dead, He sets the pattern that will follow for all believers. It was impossible for death to keep Christ – the giver and sustainer of all life. In John 1:3-4 we see clearly,

> *"Through Him all things were made; without Him nothing was made that has been made. In Him was life, and that life was the light of men."*

Jesus Christ has all authority over death, hell and the grave. The writer of Hebrews confirms the Son's role as sustainer of all creation when writing in Hebrews 1:3,

> *"The Son is the radiance of God's glory and the exact representation of his being, sustaining all things by his powerful Word. After he had provided purification for sins, he sat down at the right hand of the Majesty in heaven."*

The resurrection power of Jesus is now available to **all believers** through the ministry of the Holy Spirit. Most Christians today go through their day-to-day lives totally unaware of the power available to them. This is because many believers do not walk in the Word of God.

Paul said to Timothy in II Timothy 2:15,

> *"Do your best to present yourself to God as one approved, a workman who does not need to be*

ashamed and who correctly handles the word
of truth."

How Does the Holy Spirit Help Us?

One of The Holy Spirit's main functions is to lead and guide, "believers to all truth." (John 16:13). For the Holy Spirit to do this more fully in the life of the believer – the individual needs to have or possess more of God's Truth for this "revealing." When you and I, as believers in Jesus Christ, do our part – seeking a deeper relationship with Him through prayer and Bible study – God is always faithful to honor His Word. He wants to fully reveal His truth to those who correctly handle the Word of truth.

> *"Faith comes by hearing and hearing by the*
> *Word of Christ."*

Thus we grow in our faith as Romans 10:17 says.

The New Testament Church is Born

In this passage in Acts chapter two, we are witnessing the birth of the New Testament church. Peter is explaining the significance of Jesus' death and resurrection. He quotes King David from Psalm 16:8-11,

> *"I saw the Lord always before me. Because he*
> *is at my right hand, I will not be shaken.*

Therefore my heart is glad and my tongue rejoices; my body also will live in hope, because you will not abandon me to the grave, nor will you let your Holy One see decay. You have made known to me the paths of life; you will fill me with joy in your presence."

No wonder David's heart was glad – physical death is not the end of our existence! Jesus had promised he will "*never leave us nor forsake us*" (Hebrews 13:5). David prophesies,

"Nor will you let your Holy One see decay."

Peter explains David's prophecy in Acts 2:30-33,

"But he was a prophet and knew that God had promised him on oath that he would place one of his descendants on his throne. Seeing what was ahead, he spoke of the resurrection of the Christ, that he was not abandoned to the grave, nor did his body see decay. God raised this Jesus to life and we are all witnesses of the fact. Exalted to the right hand of God, he has received from the Father the promised Holy Spirit and has poured out what you now see and hear."

Peter is connecting the dots between the prophecy given to King David and the death and resurrection of Jesus Christ. What other explanation could there be when one witnesses the outpouring of the Holy Spirit at the day of Pentecost. Peter refers to a "promise on oath" that God made to David concerning placing one of David's descendants on his throne. This promise or oath is found in 2 Samuel 7:12-16.

Jesus Came From the Line of King David

In Matthew chapter one, we see confirmation of this connection between David and Jesus, as Matthew uses a record of genealogy from Abraham through David to Christ. David, knowing this promise from God, sees ahead as the Father fulfills his promise in the resurrection of Jesus. Jesus' body certainly did not "see decay" as he was raised to life on the third day. Peter points out clearly, "and we are all witnesses to the fact." Jesus is the "heir" of David's throne as Christ was born to the virgin, Mary, who was a descendant of David. (This "throne" or "kingdom" will be explored to a greater extent in a later chapter of this book). In Acts 2:34-35 Peter quotes David in Psalm 110:1,

> *"The Lord said to my Lord: Sit at my right hand until I make your enemies a footstool for your feet."*

Jesus, speaking of himself to the Pharisees, quotes this verse in Matthew 22:44. What David is saying is "the Lord" (God the Father) spoke to "his Lord" (the Messiah) to sit at His right hand until all Christ's enemies were made His (God's) footstool. **David recognized that his descendent would be divine – the Messiah – since the Father would resurrect him from the dead.** Not only resurrect Him but exalt Him to the seat of authority at the right hand of God as the Holy One of Israel! This exaltation of Christ to this promised position was now being affirmed and confirmed by the outpouring of the Holy Spirit on the day of Pentecost! Jesus taught concerning the coming of the Holy Spirit in John 14:26,

> *"But the Counselor, the Holy Spirit, whom the Father will send in my name, will teach you all things and will remind you of everything I have said to you."*

In John chapter sixteen, Jesus further explains in verses 7 and 13,

> *"But I tell you the truth: It is for your good that I am going away. Unless I go away, the Counselor will not come to you; but if I go, I will send him to you ... when he, the Spirit of truth comes, he will guide you into all truth. He will not speak on his own; he will speak*

only what he hears, and he will tell you what is
yet to come."

Jesus promised the coming of the Holy Counselor or Spirit. Then God delivered with the beginning of the Holy Spirit's ministry in Acts chapter two. Echoing the angel's voice at Jesus' tomb, "just as he said." One wonderful purpose of having God's written Word is that his believers can study the prophecies and fulfillments of God's promises, thus learning the most valuable lesson of life namely – Our God can be trusted in all circumstances. We can take Him at His Word! To learn of God and who He really is – we must study His Word. Jesus, teaching his disciples, confirms David's prophecy of him in John 16:27-28,

> *"... the Father himself loves you because you*
> *have loved me and have believed that I came*
> *from God. I came from the Father and entered*
> *the world; now I am leaving the world and*
> *going back to the Father."*

Phase one of the holy mission is accomplished!

Paul, teaching in 1 Corinthians 6:14, says, "By his power God raised the Lord from the dead and he will raise us also."

The resurrection of the dead had been taught for centuries before Jesus' death, resurrection and ascension. Therefore, the church at Corinth had, at least, some basic knowledge of the subject.

Yet, false teachers had come and led the people's thinking away from the truth. Paul's assignment was to help the people see the clear teaching of scripture as it related not only to Jesus' resurrection but also their own. We look into 1 Corinthians, chapter fifteen for our answers.

Paul begins in verses 3-8,

> *"For what I received I passed on to you as of first importance: that Christ died for our sins according to the Scriptures, that he was buried, that he was raised on the third day according to the scriptures and that he appeared to Peter, and then to the twelve. After that, he appeared to more than five hundred of the brothers at the same time, most of whom are still living, though some have fallen asleep. Then he appeared to James, then to all the apostles, and last of all he appeared to me also, as to one abnormally born."*

The Good News – The Gospel

In verses three and four, Paul emphasizes that what he received from the Lord and passed on to the church at Corinth was first priority – namely, the Gospel – the good news that Jesus died on a cross, was buried and raised on the third day, just as the Scriptures said. This truth makes it possible for all believers to be "raised to life". Paul continues to build his case for Christ with the facts concerning the "post-resurrection" appearance of Jesus. Starting with Peter and the apostles, Paul reminds the church of his appearing to five hundred at one time – most of whom were still living at the time of Paul's writing. The appearance to Peter is found in Luke 24:34, his appearing to the Twelve in Luke 24:36-43, and also in John 20:19-23. The reference to "Twelve" is to Jesus' apostles, yet we know that Judas had already committed suicide for his betrayal of Christ. We understand of whom Paul is speaking and have scriptural references to the, "Eleven" in Matthew 28:16. Also in Acts 1:25-26, we see the sting of Judas' betrayal is still fresh with the apostles,

> *"... to take over this apostolic ministry, which Judas left to go where he belongs. Then they cast lots, and the lot fell to Matthias; so he was added to the eleven apostles."*

I want clarity for all to see that whether Scripture refers to the "Eleven" or the "Twelve", we are still speaking of the same group.

Jesus Appears to Five Hundred

The appearance to the five hundred at the same time is found in Matthew 28 where Jesus gives the "Great Commission". Also, in Acts 1:3 Luke writes,

> *"After his suffering, he showed himself to these men and gave many convincing proofs that he was alive. He appeared to them over a period of forty days and spoke about the kingdom of God."*

All those who believe must receive God and His redemptive work on the cross by faith. Yet, our Father never expects belief based on blind faith. Thus, all the appearances are for believers to have even more proof of his victory over death.

In verse seven, we find a particularly tender scene. This James is the half brother of Jesus who did not believe in Christ before the resurrection. Even though he did not believe, Jesus still loved him and sought him out in order that James would truly see Jesus and believe. Is not that the same thing that takes place for all followers of Christ? That He loves us so much he sought us out –

> *"not wanting any to perish, but that all might come to repentance and believe"* (2 Peter 3:9).

Our God is so patient, loving and kind. He desires all people from all over the globe to come into a right relationship with Him. I know this from personal experience – because I came to trust Christ as a 21 year-old senior in college. In all honesty, I was not seeking God. My lifestyle was typical of many college students in the late seventies. Parties, friends, parties, classes, parties – you get the picture. Yet God drew me to a local congregation going through turmoil. When I went to see what the problems were – I ended up hearing the Gospel and accepted Christ. My life has never been the same! The great news is – if God did this for me, He will also do this for you by allowing circumstances to take place so that you will come to know Him!

The Last Appearance of Christ

The last appearance of Christ Paul mentions is that of his own personal encounter on the road to Damascus. The story is found in Acts 9:1-8. Here Jesus strikes Saul down off of his "ride" and removes his sight, but only to change Saul and his eternal destiny. This is a perfect picture of what takes place in a believer's conversion experience. We, like Saul, become truly new creations – the old is gone and the new has come. Paul admits his conversion was as one "abnormally born." Yet, God reaches us all through the different circumstances of our individual lives.

All Things New

Have you ever experienced the smell of a new car? A new house? New clothing? This is something we remember – yet things do not hold the "new" feel or smell forever. However, as Saul and many believers have discovered, our relationship with Christ is something genuinely new every morning. This is because God chooses to forgive our sins and not hold them against us. Through Christ's death and resurrection, we can experience ALL that God has for us now and throughout all eternity! We have reason to celebrate!

After closely examining all the evidence, Paul concludes in 1 Corinthians 15:20-23,

> *"But Christ has indeed been raised from the*
> *dead, the first fruits of those who have fallen*
> *asleep. For since death came through a man,*
> *the resurrection of the dead comes also*
> *through a man. For as in Adam all die, so in*
> *Christ all will be made alive. But each in his*
> *own turn: Christ, the first fruits; then when he*
> *comes, those who belong to him."*

This reference to "first fruits" is found in Leviticus 23: 10-11, 17, 20. ***The first fruits were a symbol of promise where the giver acknowledged that all of the harvest belonged to the Creator.*** Jesus fulfills this promise by being the first fruit raised from the dead. Lazarus and others Christ raised from the dead – lived to physically die again. But the Messiah lives forevermore. Thus, he is God the Father's guarantee for resurrection to all who are in Christ. Paul contrasts the differences between Adam and Jesus. Sin came through Adam. The forgiveness of sin comes through Jesus Christ. The wages of sin is death (Romans 6:23); therefore death came through Adam. However, life comes through Christ because of his victory over death, hell (judgment) and the grave. In verse twenty-three, Paul teaches that everyone waits his turn. Christ had to be first, thus the guarantee that all believers will be raised to new life at his second coming.

What Will Our Resurrected Bodies Be Like?

In verse thirty-five the question is raised,

> *"But someone may ask, How are the dead raised? With what kind of body will they come?"*

After correcting the Corinthians for doubting, Paul begins to explain the believer's resurrection body. He gives several examples from agriculture. In verse thirty-six, Paul begins

> *"What you sow does not come to life unless it dies. When you sow, you do not plant the body that will be, but just a seed, perhaps of wheat or something else. But God gives it a body as*

he has determined, and to each kind of seed he gives its own body."

The teaching here is clear – just as we would plant a garden in the spring time, the seed planted must die in order for "new life" to come forth. God gives each a body as he determined before the creation of the world. For example, the kernel of planted corn grows into a stalk with a brand new ear. So many things God wants to teach us – we already can see! Paul continues in verses thirty-nine and forty to give examples of different kinds of bodies – human, animals, birds and fish. Heavenly bodies and these earthly bodies–

> *"...but the splendor of the heavenly bodies is one kind, and the splendor of the earthly bodies is another. The sun has one kind of splendor, the moon another and the stars another; and star differs from star in splendor."*

Paul is laying the foundation for believers to have a basic understanding of our resurrected bodies. Just as our earthly bodies were created for our time and life on earth, our "heavenly" or resurrected bodies were created and will be suited for our new life in eternity – serving, worshipping and living in the presence of God! In Revelation 21:4-5a John writes of God,

"He will wipe every tear from their eyes. There will be no more death or mourning or crying or pain, for the old order of things has passed away. He who was seated on the throne said, I am making everything new!"

Paul continues this awesome teaching concerning the transition of our earthly bodies to our eternal bodies in verse forty-two:

"So will it be with the resurrection of the dead. The body that is sown is perishable, it is raised imperishable; it is sown in dishonor, it is raised in glory; it is sown in weakness, it is raised in power; it is sown a natural body, it is raised a spiritual body."

Look at the wording or grouping of words – perishable, dishonor, weakness, natural. We can add a word that caused this condition – sin. Contrast that condition and those words with imperishable, glory, power, and spiritual. All of these are made possible by the death and resurrection of Jesus Christ! He removed all the sin that causes the condition of the first group of words, thus enabling and allowing us to step into the second group of words which describe briefly how we will live throughout all eternity! If you are still wondering about your resurrected body, just look to

Jesus as your example. In his appearances, that we have already discussed, He walked, talked, ate, enjoyed his relationships with his followers and taught them further about the Kingdom of God for forty days! This is a brief clue that in eternity we will enjoy life as God intended – totally free from sin, death, mourning, and pain. We will enjoy fellowship with all those in Christ whom we know and love. It will be the most incredible "family reunion" we have ever experienced! Scripture teaches,

> *"No eye has seen, no ear has heard, no mind has conceived what God has prepared for those who love him – but God has revealed it to us by his Spirit"* (1 Corinthians 2:9-10).

The Holy Spirit was sent by Jesus to lead us and guide us to all truth (John 16:13). That phrase "all truth" is not limited to this life and this earth only.

My prayer for you is that God will place in you a hunger and thirst for Him and His righteousness like you have never experienced before!

Paul further contrasts beginning in verse forty-four,

> *"If there is a natural body, there is also a spiritual body. So it is written: The first man Adam became a living being, the last Adam, a life-giving spirit. The spiritual did not come*

first, but the natural and after that the spiritual. The first man was of the dust of the earth the second man from heaven. As was the earthly man, so are those who are of the earth; and as is the man from heaven, so also are those who are of heaven. And just as we have borne the likeness of the earthly man, so shall we bear the likeness of the man from heaven."

All human beings bear the physical likeness of the first Adam. We are all physically born into the family of man. Therefore, for human beings to be made into the spiritual likeness of the second Adam, Christ, they MUST BE BORN AGAIN. As Nicodemus discovered, this transformation is not physical or mental or just emotional. It is spiritual. If we follow the first Adam's example we will fall to our sin and die. Yet, by following (accepting, believing, receiving) the second Adam, the one from heaven, we will be cleansed from our sin and live with Him forever. We receive this spiritual body at his second appearing.

In 1 Corinthians 15:50-53, Paul teaches,

"I declare to you, brothers, that flesh and blood cannot inherit the kingdom of God, nor does the perishable inherit the imperishable. Listen, I tell you a mystery: We will not all

sleep, but we will all be changed – in a flash, in the twinkling of an eye, at the last trumpet. For the trumpet will sound, the dead will be raised imperishable, and we will be changed. For the perishable must clothe itself with the imperishable, and the mortal with immortality."

Paul is laying out a foundation of understanding of the transition that must take place for the believer to receive his/her "glorified" body. Do not think it strange that he would use the word "mystery". The usage here refers to a truth that was not understood or known, but which has been revealed. As we have previously discussed – the perishable body is our earthly body. Due to sin, it has a beginning and an end. It is perishable. We exchange our physical body – the perishable, for the eternal body – the imperishable. This body does not perish, for we will live forever in the presence of the Lord.

But when? The answer is found in verse fifty-two, *"at the last trumpet."* The dead will be raised imperishable, their earthly bodies, probably already decayed, will be raised just like Jesus' resurrected body! This is exactly what Jesus said in Matthew 24:31,

"And he (Son of Man) will send his angels with a loud trumpet call, and they will gather his

*elect from the four winds, from one end of the
heavens to the other."*

This is the great scene on planet earth when the true
believers will be "snatched away" or "raptured". (We will go into
greater detail on this topic later). In John 5:25, Jesus speaks of this
truth,

> *"I tell you the truth, a time is coming and has
> now come when the dead will hear the voice of
> the Son of God and those who hear will live."*

Paul sums up this section of his teaching on the subject in
verses 54-58: He writes,

> *"When the perishable has been clothed with
> the imperishable, and the mortal with
> immortality, then the saying that is written
> will come true: Death has been swallowed up
> in victory. Where, O death, is your victory?
> Where, O death, is your sting? The sting of
> death is sin, and the power of sin is the law.
> But thanks be to God! He gives us the victory
> through our Lord Jesus Christ. Therefore, my
> dear brothers, stand firm. Let nothing move
> you. Always give yourselves fully to the work*

of the Lord, because you know that your labor
in the Lord is not in vain."

When Will the Rapture Take Place?

In verse fifty-four, the key question is <u>when?</u> Paul confirms that at the point when the believer receives his/her resurrected body - this is the very moment when these two prophecies of Isaiah 25:8 (verse fifty-four) and Hosea 13:14 (verse fifty-five) will be fulfilled. We have already answered the larger "when" question – as verse fifty-two states "in a flash, in the twinkling of any eye – at the last trumpet." This last trumpet is when the believers, both dead and alive, will be resurrected or be given their "glorified" bodies. At that glorious moment for the believer, "death will be truly swallowed up in victory." The sting of death and sin will be no more. There will be no more power in sin.

In verse fifty-seven, Paul exclaims,

> *"But thanks be to God! He gives us the victory*
> *through our Lord Jesus Christ."*

This awesome victory is an eternal victory! No more death, sin, pain, mourning, tears. Based on this magnificent eternal victory we believers can "stand firm" (verse fifty-eight). Nothing Satan throws at us can move us! This is why we devote our lives, resources, energies, and ambitions to the "work of the Lord."

Because we know that our labor for Him is never in vain. One remarkable promise is found in Revelation 20:6, where John writes,

> *"Blessed and holy are those who have part in the first resurrection. The second death has no power over them, but they will be priests of God and of Christ and will reign with him for a thousand years."*

Paul reminds us in Philippians 3:20-21:

> *"But our citizenship is in heaven. And we eagerly await a Savior from there, the Lord Jesus Christ, who, by the power that enables him to bring everything under his control, will transform our lowly bodies so that they will be like his glorious body."*

We, as His followers, need to believe and receive these and all of God's great promises to

> *"those who love him and are called according to his purpose"* (Romans 8:28).

The Ascension of Jesus Christ

Our final focus of the first coming of Jesus Christ concerns his "return" to the Father. Jesus speaks of his ascension on several occasions in John's Gospel (John 7:33; John 8:21; John 14:23, 28; John 16:5-10, 16, 17-28; John 17:11,13). Accounts of "the ascension" are found in Luke 24:50-52 and Acts 1: 9-11. First, the account from Luke:

> *"When he had led them out of the vicinity of Bethany, he lifted up his hands and blessed them. While he was blessing them, he left them and was taken up into heaven. Then they worshipped him and returned to Jerusalem with great joy".*

Based on this truth the writer of Hebrews encourages us in 4:14,

> *"Therefore, since we have a great high priest who has gone through the heavens, Jesus the Son of God, let us hold firmly to the faith we profess."*

Peter, an eyewitness of the event, speaks of Jesus in 1 Peter 3:22,

> *"who has gone into heaven and is at God's right hand – with angels, authorities and powers in submission to him."*

John, another eyewitness of the ascension writes prophetically in Revelation 12:5,

> *"She gave birth to a son, a male child, who will rule all the nations with an iron scepter. And her child was snatched up to God and to his throne."*

This "snatching up" is a beautiful description of Jesus' exit from planet earth. Returning to the Acts 1:9-11 account – we discover a most valuable truth in our pursuit of knowledge of Christ's **second coming**. Luke wrote,

> *"After he said this, he was taken up before their very eyes, and a cloud hid him from their sight. They were looking intently up into the sky as he was going, when suddenly two men dressed in white stood beside them. 'Men of Galilee,' they said, 'why do you stand here looking into the sky? This same Jesus, who has been taken from you into heaven, will come back in the same way you have seen him go into heaven.'"*

The angels announced his birth. An angel was there to proclaim the resurrection. Two angels are present at his ascension, and an angel will sound the loud trumpet call to signal his second coming. He will not come back as the "meek and mild" Savior, but truly as the "Lord of Lords and King of Kings," to "rule all the nations with an iron scepter." "Amen. Come Lord Jesus" (Revelation 22:20b).

PART II

THE SECOND COMING OF

CHRIST

CHAPTER 6

THE SIGNS OF HIS COMING

(MATTHEW 24:1-22)

When one approaches the subject of the awaited coming of Christ, where does one begin? Where is the best starting point? In my thirty years of walking with Jesus – I have discovered that it is always best to start with what *He* taught about the topic. The Second Coming of Christ is a widely discussed topic today, and, as we will discover, has been since Jesus' ascension.

One final warning – let us not hear only what we *want* to hear from the Bible – let us truly hear what God is saying to His people through His Word.

Our journey starts in Matthew, chapter twenty four. His disciples ask Him privately to,

> *"Tell us, they said when will this happen, and*
> *what will be the sign of your coming and the*
> *end of the age?"(Matthew 24:3).*

111

What sparked the question was Jesus' comment in verse two, from Matthew 25:1-2,

> *"Jesus left the temple and was walking away when his disciples came up to him to call his attention to it's buildings. 'Do you see all these things?' he asked, 'I tell you the truth, not one stone here will be left on another; every one will be thrown down.'"*

The disciples, in calling Jesus' attention to the magnificent structure of the temple and its buildings, are in essence confessing that they cannot fathom a fulfillment of Matthew 23:38, which reads, *"Lord, your house is left to you desolate."* This passage refers to Jeremiah's prophecy that the Lord expects obedience or this *"palace will become ruin"* (Jeremiah 22:6). The disciples could not imagine God allowing His beautiful temple to be destroyed. Keep in mind, the first century Jew's version of Messiah was one that would come in the name of the Lord and rule the nations politically on planet earth. Jesus asks the disciples in verse two, *"Do you see these things?"* He wanted to be certain that they were seeing the same structure of which he was speaking. According to Josephus, in his work *Antiquities*, the massive stones "were white, some were 37 feet long, 12 feet high and 18 feet wide."[1] Herod's temple, the third Jewish center of worship, stood fifteen stories high. No wonder these men could not begin to think that a day was coming when God's temple would be desolate! We might understand how they felt when we recall most of the world was similarly shocked and astonished at the fall of the "Twin Towers" in New York City on 9-11-01.

Jesus' words came true in 70 A.D when the Roman general Titus besieged Jerusalem and completely and utterly destroyed the city, the temple and everything contained therein. "Stones were even pried apart to collect the gold leaf that melted from the roof when the temple was set on fire. Excavations in 1968 uncovered large numbers of these stones, toppled from the walls by the invaders".[2] God's Word is true – both historically and prophetically. Stop and think about this point – when Jesus spoke these words, the event had not yet taken place. In addition, archeological excavation centuries after the fact, proves for all to see the accuracy of Christ's words!

Another important point is the timing of these "end time" events. Jesus said in Matthew 24:36,

> *"No one knows about that day or hour, not*
> *even the angels in heaven, nor the Son, but*
> *only the Father."*

This truth is also found in Mark 13:32. Just as we do not know the day and hour of our death – we do not know the specific day and time Jesus will return. We are to live by faith not by sight. Thus, knowing the precise moment of the return of the Son of Man would be a stumbling block to "true" faith. Jesus modeled how his followers should live – by faith and obedience to the Father. When asked about restoring the kingdom to Israel (the Second Coming of Jesus) in Acts 1:6-8, Jesus responded,

> *"It is not for you to know the times or dates the Father has set by his own authority. But you will receive power when the Holy Spirit comes on you; and you will be my witnesses in Jerusalem, and in all Judea and Samaria, and to the ends of the earth."*

This passage is a clear instruction from Jesus to his followers – Do not be sitting around marking time and speculating about his return. Go out in the power of the Holy Spirit and be his witnesses. The true church is to be about the Father's business just as He modeled in his earthly ministry.

We also need to qualify the term "last days". The apostles taught that the "last days" began with Jesus' first coming and will close with his return. For example, Peter, in Acts 2:17, explaining the coming of the Holy Spirit at Pentecost, quotes the prophet Joel (Joel 2:28), *"In the last days, God says, I will pour out my Spirit on all people."* We will look deeper into Joel's prophecy later. But Peter views the coming of the Holy Spirit as a "last days" event! Paul, instructing young Timothy in 2 Timothy 3:1-5, writes,

"But mark this: There will be terrible times in the last days. People will be lovers of themselves, lovers of money, boastful, proud, abusive, disobedient of their parents, ungrateful, unholy, without love, unforgiving, slanderous, without self control, brutal, not lovers of the good, treacherous, rash, conceited, lovers of pleasure rather than lovers of God – having a form of godliness but denying its power. Have nothing to do with them."

On one hand it seems Paul has been reading headlines from our current newspapers – maybe even visiting our churches. Yet, he instructs Timothy to "have nothing to do with these people." Paul clearly realized the "last days" had already begun.

In 1 Peter 4:7, the apostle reminds his readers,

"The end of all things is near. Therefore, be clear minded and self controlled so that you can pray".

Peter also points out in 2 Peter 3:3,

"First of all, you must understand that in the last days scoffers will come, scoffing and following their own evil desires."

He is warning his readers in this passage that these scoffers were already present and doing their best to discourage Christ's followers of his second coming.

John writes in 1 John 2:18,

> *"Dear children, this is the true last hour; and as you have heard that the antichrist is coming, even now many antichrists have come. This is how we know it is the last hour."*

Here, John warns his readers not only of the coming "beast", but the many who oppose Christ and his followers then. The writer of Hebrews recognized the times also in Hebrews 1:1-2,

> *"In the past God spoke to our forefathers through the prophets at many times in various ways, but in these last days he has spoken to us by his Son, whom he appointed heir of all things, and through whom he made the universe."*

My encouragement here is for us to allow the Holy Spirit to influence our thinking by studying the Word, thus giving Him a foundation on which to build His truth in our lives. In Matthew 24:4, Jesus answers the question of *"what will be the sign of your coming and of the end of the age?" (Matthew 24:3b).*

Jesus answered,

"Watch out that no one deceives you. For many will come in my name, claiming 'I am the Christ,' and will deceive many. You will hear of wars and rumors of wars, but see to it that you are not alarmed. Such things must happen, but the end is still to come. Nation will rise against nation, and kingdom against kingdom. There will be famines and earthquakes in various places. All these are the beginning of birth pains" (Matthew 24:4-8).

As an unlearned observer, one could say, "We have had all these things happening since the beginning of time – even well before Jesus' first coming!" Peter warns scoffers of all generations in 2 Peter 3:4-7,

"They will say, 'Where is this coming he promised? Ever since our fathers died, everything goes on as it has since the beginning of creation.' But they deliberately forget that long ago by God's word the

heavens existed and the earth was formed out of water and by water. By these waters also the world of that time was deluged and destroyed. By the same word the present heavens and earth are reserved for fire, being kept for the Day of Judgment and destruction of ungodly men."

It is not a matter of *if*, but of *when*! Not *when* as in times or dates – but a matter of timing – namely God's perfect timing. Peter goes on to explain why Jesus has yet to return to judge the nations in 2 Peter 3:9-10,

"The Lord is slow in keeping his promise, as some understand slowness. He is patient with you, not wanting anyone to perish, but everyone to come to repentance. But the day of the Lord will come like a thief."

Peter is echoing Christ's warning in Matthew – "Watch out that no one deceives you." Jesus' first sign is the spiritual deception of false christs, false teachers and false prophets. This will eventually lead up to the greatest of all false christs – the beast of Revelation 13 and Daniel 7, 9. The second sign of Christ's warning is the "grab for political power and control" in the "wars and rumors of wars." Jesus even adds a word of encouragement to "see to it that you are not alarmed." This is so key for the believer to remember – God knows all these happenings. He knows all of Satan's plans and schemes and he knows about all the evil lined up against Him! And Great News – Our God has everything under control! I want to encourage you as well, because so many people in the church today look at this scene that Jesus is describing with fear and trepidation. We, as followers of Jesus Christ, should rejoice as the Psalmist did in Psalm 121:1-2,

> "I lift up my eyes to the hills. Where does my help come from? My help comes from the Lord, the Maker of heaven and earth."

Jesus, in Luke 21:28, says,

> "When these things begin to take place, stand up and lift up your heads, because your redemption is drawing near."

The hour of our redemption draws near as we see "these things beginning to take place."

Let's look again at Matthew 24:7 – Jesus speaks of "famines and earthquakes in various places."

Our scientists, climatologists and other weather experts point out what seems an ever-increasing number of earthquakes and natural disasters. The disastrous 2004 Tsunami in the Pacific is an example. As we have now seen by news footage and video cameras – the absolute destruction that came – seemingly without any hint or warning. Of course wars and natural disasters cause destruction of farmland and labor, which causes famines in various places of the earth. And yes, mankind has seen a variety of these things down through the ages. Yet, the key word in Matthew 24:8, that most miss entirely is ALL. Jesus said in this verse, "*All these are the beginning of birth pains.*" All of these – not collectively taking place throughout history, but when "all these" signs are taking place simultaneously – the believer needs to heed this warning as the "beginning of the birth pains." Anyone familiar with child birth knows that the start of contractions does not mean the baby is arriving now. It is a sign that the birthing process is now under way – the baby will be here soon. Jesus gives us this basic analogy of life in order for us to understand that his coming to bring eternal life is soon approaching. He again comforts us in verse six:

> "*see to it that you are not alarmed. Such things must happen, but the end is still to come.*"

Hopefully, the picture is starting to become clearer. When the believer witnesses "all these things" happening at the same time, he/she knows to "lift up your heads, because your redemption draws near." And as "our redemption draws near" – so does our Redeemer!

One key teaching point of the "end-time" prophecy is that ***our God wants us to know and understand the sign, or collective***

signs, as the Bible clearly teaches. We, if we are to truly understand, must allow Scripture to interpret Scripture. I fully realize that I have touched on this truth several times in earlier chapters. But I do not apologize for the repetition. We all need to hear and practice this principle over and over until it is the only way we study and apply God's Word. Man's opinions and viewpoints are fallible – God's Word is NOT!

Looking into the next passage in Matthew twenty-four, we see Jesus opening the window of truth a little further. In verses 9-14, Jesus says,

> *"Then you will be handed over to be persecuted and put to death, and you will be hated by all nations because of me. At that time many will turn away from the faith and will betray and hate each other, and many false prophets will appear and deceive many people. Because of the increase of wickedness, the love of most will grow cold, but he who stands firm to the end will be saved. And this Gospel of the kingdom will be preached in the whole world as a testimony to all nations, and then the end will come."*

In verse nine, *"then you will be handed over to be persecuted and put to death and you will be hated by all nations because of me."*

Some in the church today teach that Matthew twenty-four is solely for the Jews alive during the "Great Seven Year Tribulation." However, the Orthodox Jew will still be looking for Messiah at that point in time. Jesus is clearly teaching his followers that "antichrist" and his authorities are going to persecute and even put to death those who name the name of Christ! Even though Jews have been hated by much of the world, particularly by many Muslim sects – this verse has NO reference to the persecution of Jews. It has every reference to Christians being "persecuted and hated by all nations because of me." In other words, "persecuted, put to death and hated" because of their allegiance to the Lord Jesus Christ! In John 15:18, 20b, 21, Jesus says,

> *"If the world hates you, keep in mind that it hated me first... If they persecuted me, they will persecute you also ... They will treat you this way because of my name, for they do not know the One who sent me." Jesus further states in John 16:2, "They will put you out of the synagogue; in fact, a time is coming when anyone who kills you will think he is offering a service to God."*

Here Jesus is sharing of the rejection the first century Jews had for him and all those who followed him then. However, he is also teaching those who would follow him years, decades and centuries in the future. Saul, in Acts 9 had to be struck blind for Christ to get his attention concerning his persecution. Therefore, those Christians alive in the "end of the age" should expect nothing less. We believers, particularly in America, have been "sold a bill of goods" about "it's our right to be rich, loved, famous, safe from all problems, etc." These are lies from Satan. We need to heed Jesus' words in Matthew 24:4,

"Watch out that no one deceives you."

This truth in Matthew 24:9 is also supported by the Old Testament prophet Daniel. This great man of God was in the midst of his own persecution, living in exile in Babylon. Daniel predicts in chapter 7:21-22 concerning his dream,

> *"As I watched, this horn was waging war against the saints and defeating them, until the Ancient of Days came and pronounced judgment in favor of the saints of the Most High, and the time came when they possessed the kingdom."*

We will dig deeper into Daniel's writings in a coming chapter. However, there are several important points from these two verses. The horn spoken in verse twenty-one is the antichrist. Daniel 7:25 supports this,

"He will speak against the Most High and oppress his saints and try to change the set times and the laws. The saints will be handed over to him for a time, times and half a time."

Keep in mind that Daniel is writing over five hundred years before the first coming of Jesus! Here, Daniel, a Jew, writes about a group of people he calls "saints". The term "saint," according to Funk and Wagnall's New College Standard Dictionary, is defined as "a holy, godly or sanctified person; in the New Testament, any Christian believer."[3]

How in the world was Daniel, an exiled Jew, writing five hundred years before Christ, using the term "saint"? Our God amazes us once again! He gave Daniel, by way of a dream, the exact term "saints", that would be used in reference to those faithful followers of Christ whom Jesus is teaching concerning the signs of the end of the age in Matthew 24:9!

The scene Daniel sees is this "horn waging war against the saints and defeating them" is supported by Revelation 6:9-11, John writes,

"When he (the lamb in Revelation 6:1) opened the fifth seal, I saw under the altar the souls of those who had been slain because of the word of God and the testimony they had maintained. They called out in a loud voice,

124

'How long, Sovereign Lord, holy and true, until you judge the inhabitants of the earth and avenge our blood?' Then each one of them was given a white robe, and they were told to wait a little longer, until the number of their fellow servants and brothers who were to be killed as they had been was completed."

Unmistakably, John sees in his prophecy the same scenario Daniel saw in his, and both support Jesus' own prophecy that his followers would be "handed over to be persecuted and put to death . . . hated by all nations because of me" (Matthew 24:9). One could argue that Jesus' Matthew 24 teaching was just for the disciples to explain what kind of death they would have to endure. However, that does not add up since the question raised is one about the "sign of the end of the age." Not the sign of the close of the first century, not the sign of the first millennia, but the sign of the close of the "church age," when God's judgment against all those who rejected his Son will began to take place.

Daniel's "horn waging war against the saints" or followers of Christ is not a reference only to Jews. At no time in human history have Orthodox Jews been called "saints." Only when a Jew in the first century, New Testament church – after receiving Christ as Savior – would he or she been termed a "saint." To be a New Testament "saint" today or at any time, one must be a follower of Jesus. This is the same regardless whether one is a Jew or Gentile. Paul writes in Romans 10:12-13,

> "For there is no difference between Jew and Gentile – the same Lord is Lord of all and richly blesses all who call on him, for Everyone who calls on the name of the Lord will be saved."

Therefore, Daniel's usage of the term saint refers to "those who follow Jesus Christ."

John's view,

> "I saw under the altar the souls of those who had been slain because of the word of God and the testimony they had maintained",

firmly supports Jesus' Matthew 24:9 teaching. John is quick to point out these people were killed because "the word of God and their testimony." Both of these terms are New Testament figures of speech. Both relate to the "true church." Both speak of Jesus – The Word (John 1:1), and the believer's word of praise to God (testimony). The writer of Hebrews encourages us in 10:39,

> "But we are not of those who shrink back and are destroyed, but of those who believe and are saved."

Jesus' message to the churches in Revelation 2 and 3 is clear, "The blessings of heaven and eternal joys and promises of God belong to him who overcomes." Jesus encourages in Matthew 24:13,

> *"...but he who stands firm to the end will be saved." In spite of the dark times in verses 10-12, "At that time many will turn away from the faith and will betray and hate each other, and many false prophets will appear and deceive many people. Because of the increase of wickedness, the love of most will grow cold."*

Jesus says to his people, "Stand firm!" In other words, "Stay close to me; I am your shepherd. Keep your eyes on me. False prophets are coming – Don't believe them! False teachings are going to be everywhere, even in my church! Don't believe them!" We can only stand firm by staying faithful, by studying his Word, praying daily, worshipping regularly – in essence – seeking his face everyday!

Jesus is not finished teaching about the signs of the end of the age. In this next passage, we discover a central truth in Matthew 24:15. Jesus is speaking,

> *"So when you see standing in the holy place the abomination that causes desolation,*

spoken of through the prophet Daniel – let the
reader understand ..."

I believe this verse is the central teaching of Jesus' message to his followers in Matthew 24, which is the central teaching of Scripture on the signs of the end times. If you and I do not receive anything else in this writing, please "let the reader understand," hear and understand the Biblical significance of the "abomination that causes desolation."

Jesus' reference in Matthew 24:15 is to Daniel 9:25-27:

"Know and understand this: From the issuing
of the decree to restore and rebuild Jerusalem
until the Anointed One, the ruler, comes, there
will be seven "sevens," and sixty-two "sevens."
It will be rebuilt with streets and trench, but in
times of trouble. After the sixty-two "sevens,"
the Anointed One will be cut off and will have
nothing. The people of the ruler who will come
will destroy the city and the sanctuary. The
end will come like a flood: War will continue
until the end, and desolations have been
decreed. He will confirm a covenant with
many for one "seven". In the middle of the
"seven" he will put an end to sacrifice and
offering. And on a wing of the temple, he will

set up an abomination that causes desolation,
until the end that is decreed is poured out on
him."

I find it more than just interesting that Daniel says the same thing Jesus said when the prophet opens this passage with, "know and understand this." Daniel wants the believer who reads his prophecy to know and understand. He gives a specific time frame

"from the issuing of the decree to restore and
rebuild Jerusalem until the Anointed One, the
ruler, comes, there will be seven "sevens," and
sixty-two "sevens."

This is a specific time between Nehemiah's call from God to rebuild the temple and city of Jerusalem, and the public ministry of Jesus Christ. The time is actually sixty-nine times seven, or four hundred and eighty-three years. Whether we consider Nehemiah's commission as the starting point of Daniel's first 69 sevens or the letter to Ezra the priest from Persian King Artaxerxes 1 as the starting point, it is remarkably close to the years of Jesus' public ministry. Even choosing the solar calendar dates or the lunar calendar dates we see a time frame that fits Daniel's "seven sevens and sixty-two sevens."

The phrase in the last part of Daniel 9:25,

"It will be rebuilt with streets and a trench,
but in the times of trouble" is clarified in
Nehemiah 4:15-18:

"When our enemies heard that we were aware
of their plot and that God had frustrated it, we
all returned to the wall, each to his own work.
From that day on, half of my men did the
work, while the other half were equipped with
spears, shields, bows and armor. The officers
posted themselves behind all the people of
Judah who were building the wall. Those who
carried materials did their work with one
hand and held a weapon in the other, and
each of the builders wore his sword at this side
as he worked."

God's work has always had opposition or "times of trouble."
It is no different today as we witness, seemingly all over the globe,
Satan opposing the work of God's Anointed One.

Daniel 9:26a,

"After the sixty-two sevens, the Anointed One
will be cut off and will have nothing."

This prophecy is a direct reference to the crucifixion of Jesus
Christ. The time frame is this: the seven "sevens" is the time God

130

gave the children of Israel to complete his task of restoring/rebuilding the temple in Jerusalem. The sixty-two "sevens" is the time between the completion of the temple and the death of Messiah on the cross. The usage of the term "Anointed One" is consistently used to describe the one who will come in the Name of the Lord to save Israel and the nations from their sin. In Isaiah 61:1-2, the prophet writes of Messiah,

> *"The Spirit of the Sovereign Lord is on me, because the Lord has anointed me to preach good news to the poor. He has sent me to bind up the brokenhearted, to proclaim freedom for the captives and release from darkness for the prisoners, to proclaim the year of the Lord's favor...."*

Jesus applies this passage to Himself in Luke 4:17-19,

> *"The scroll of the prophet Isaiah was handed to him. Unrolling it, he found the place where it is written: 'The Spirit of the Lord is on me, because he has anointed me to preach good news to the poor. He has sent me to proclaim freedom for the prisoners and recovery of sight for the blind, to release the oppressed, to proclaim the year of the Lord's favor"*

Daniel's phrase "and will have nothing" demonstrates to all that Jesus' first coming was as Savior of the world (John 3:16), which did not include an earthly kingship. Yet, his Second Coming will consummate his Lordship over all the nations – Israel included.

Daniel 9:26b,

> *"The people of the ruler who will come will destroy the city and the sanctuary."*

The Romans are the "people of the ruler" and as I have already pointed out in 70 A.D. destroyed Jerusalem and the temple built by Herod. The worship of Roman emperors is a preview of the "antichrist" and his demands during the seven-year tribulation. "These Roman rulers who set themselves up as gods and demanded to be worshipped by the people while still alive, were first century emperors like Caligula, Nero and Domitian. These leaders were simply following the long-established practice of ascribing divinity to rulers, as the Roman senate started the emperor cult by deifying, after their deaths, Augustus and subsequent emperors who had served well."[3] Caligula, Nero and Domitian took emperor worship to a new level by demanding worship from their subjects while still living. This sets up verse twenty-seven. However, the last part of verse twenty-six needs our attention.

Daniel 9:26b,

"The end will come like a flood: War will continue until the end, and desolations have been decreed."

In all my years of studying end time prophecy, I have discovered that there is a short-term view and a long-term view. In verse twenty-six alone, Daniel's prophecy spans over twenty centuries. We have already discussed the fact that God's *timing* is always perfect. He is not restrained nor constrained by time – He is its author! Daniel gives the reader a sweeping panorama, from Ezra and Nehemiah rebuilding the temple to Jesus Christ's first coming and crucifixion, to the Roman destruction of Jerusalem and the temple in 70 A.D. right through to the "end" where war continues "until the desolations have been decreed." Make no mistake – this phrase "desolations that have been decreed" is when God has finally had enough and pours out his judgment on Satan, the "Beast" or "antichrist," the false prophet and all those who have rejected Jesus Christ as the Son of God!

Now we can look into Daniel 9:27,

"He will confirm a covenant with many for one "seven." In the middle of the "seven" he will put an end to sacrifice and offering. And on a wing of the temple, he will set up an abomination that causes desolation until the end that is decreed is poured out on him."

First, I want to dispel a false assumption some have made by teaching that the "He" at the opening of the verse refers to Christ. I can see an Orthodox Jew, who is presently looking for Messiah to appear, to falsely presume this. However, even under "light" Biblical scrutiny we can clearly see that Daniel is speaking of the "antichrist." This is how we can determine that this "He" is not Jesus Christ: Would Jesus – teaching in Matthew 24:15 – warn his followers about himself being the abomination that causes desolation? How absurd! I will go further and say that those who teach that Daniel 9:27 describes Jesus are the true abomination because they mislead others and blaspheme God's Son. Jesus never confirmed a covenant with many for seven years. his covenant is forever! It is eternal. Jesus did not put an end to the sacrifice and offering in the middle of the seven – He ended it with His sacrificial death on the cross as the true Lamb of God! Jesus did not set himself upon the wing of the temple – He, as King of kings and Lord of lords, belongs in the Holy of Holies! There is no decree, no abomination, no desolation – no evil plot that can defeat Him! Daniel speaks of Christ in Daniel 7:14,

> "He was given authority, glory and sovereign power; all peoples, nations and men of every language worshipped him. His dominion is an everlasting dominion that will not pass away, and his kingdom is one that will never be destroyed."

Jesus is certainly not the "he" in the beginning of this verse.

Now for the true identity of this "he" -- Daniel explains: "he will confirm a covenant with many for "seven". This act opens the "Great Seven Year Tribulation" period. The covenant he signs or confirms will be with Jews and other nations. The Orthodox Jew presently living in Jerusalem is longing to worship according to the Old Testament laws in the temple. When "he" – the antichrist appears on the world scene, probably as a politician or diplomat, and signs an agreement allowing the Jews to institute "sacrifice and offering" - many will be deceived just as Jesus warns in Matthew 24. As of this writing, the Orthodox Jew living in Jerusalem has no temple in which to worship. The temple destroyed in 70 AD needs to be rebuilt or replaced. These conservative Jews want this temple rebuilt on the "Temple Mount". One major problem – the temple mount presently has a Muslim Mosque on it, the "Dome of the Rock". Therefore, we can clearly see that a major "covenant", treaty, "peace pact," or agreement is going to have to be negotiated by a very powerful, skillful diplomat who promises much good to all in the "covenant".

However, "in the middle of the seven he will put an end to sacrifice and offering." This world leader – the antichrist – will break his word and break the agreement. Keep in mind that Daniel is speaking/writing to his people the Jews (Daniel 9:24). Please remember that the passage in which Jesus teaches about the end times is found in Matthew's Gospel in the New Testament. The writer, Matthew, was a former tax collector – hated by his own people, the Jews, for betraying them by working for the godless Romans, taxing and stealing from his own people. Therefore, Matthew, as a disciple of Messiah, compiles Christ's teaching to help his people see that Jesus is the Holy One sent from the Father. "His" Gospel is distinctively Jewish as he wrote in a style that Jews would hear God's message and could understand that Messiah has come.

Not only does "he" (antichrist) break his word, but he does the unthinkable by demanding to be worshipped, according to Daniel 9:27c:

> *"And on a wing of the temple, he will set up an abomination that causes desolation, until the end that is decreed is poured out on him."*

This same antichrist is also described in Daniel 11:31-32:

> *"His armed forces will rise up to desecrate the temple fortress and will abolish the daily sacrifice. Then they will set up the abomination that causes desolation. With flattery he will corrupt those who have violated the covenant, but the people who know their God will firmly resist him."*

The Apostle Paul writes in 2 Thessalonians 2:4,

"He will oppose and will exalt himself over everything that is called God or is worshipped, so that he sets himself up in God's temple, proclaiming himself to be God."

This 2 Thessalonians verse is key, since historically we know that Antiochus Epiphanes in 168 BC plundered the temple and erected an altar to a pagan god Zeus. Paul is writing this letter to the church at Thessalonica in the early fifties of the first century. Therefore, Paul is writing of a future time and future leader – he would certainly not have been referring to Antiochus Epiphanes' desecration of the temple over two hundred years earlier. Another solid teaching point is that God uses the Old Testament as a preview or precursor of the New Testament or future person, place or event. John writes of the antichrist and his false prophet in Revelation 13:13-15:

"And he performed great and miraculous signs, even causing fire to come down from heaven to earth in full view of men. Because of the signs he was given power to do on behalf of the first beast, he deceived the inhabitants of the earth. He ordered them to set up an image in honor of the beast who was wounded by the sword and yet lived. He was given power to give breath to the image of the first

beast, so that it could speak and cause all who refused to worship the image to be killed."

No wonder Jesus repeated strongly several times, "Do not be deceived." Believers in that day will have to stay close to Christ in their daily walk so as not to be fooled by Satan's deception.

This "abomination" is obviously the act of any one setting themselves up as God in his holy temple. We can distinguish this action that "causes desolation" from the similar acts throughout history because Jesus Christ is teaching us concerning the end times in Matthew 24:15. Without Jesus warning us in Scripture, we could wrongfully apply Daniel 9:27 to several evil leaders throughout history – Antiochus Epiphanes being one in 168 BC. However, the context is the end of human history, as we know it. Remember the disciples question to Jesus concerning, *"What will be the sign of your coming and the end of the age?"*

Finally, let us consider the last phrase, "until the end that is decreed is poured out on him." We believers sometimes live our lives as if God is "asleep at the wheel". The "abomination that causes desolation" has not and will not take our God by surprise. As a matter of fact, look at the final phrase of Daniel 9:27, "until the end that is decreed." Not only will this abomination not take God by surprise, He has already decreed the precise end in Scripture! The wording "end that is decreed" is in the past-perfect tense. In other words, the "end that is decreed" is just as if it had already taken place. The "end that is decreed" for Satan, antichrist, the false prophet and all who mock and reject Jesus Christ, is a done deal. For when God Almighty decrees something, it is as good as done.

In the verses that immediately follow Jesus' warning in Matthew 24:15, we see the destruction of Jerusalem. Following the antichrist's abomination, Jesus says,

> *"let those who are in Judea flee to the mountains. Let no one on the roof of his house go down to take anything out of the house. Let no one in the field go back to get his cloak. How dreadful it will be in those days for pregnant women and nursing mothers! Pray that your flight will not take place in winter or on the Sabbath. For then there will be great distress, unequaled from the beginning of the world until now – and never to be equaled again. If those days had not been cut short, no one would survive, but for the sake of the elect those days will be shortened."*

In verse sixteen, we hear Jesus warn those living in Judea to "run for the hills." Why are they to run? Because "antichrist" is demanding all to worship him or be put to death (Revelation 13:13-15) as John's writing explains. It will be such a desperate time that anyone "on the roof" or outside their home should leave their belongings and flee! Just like in the days of the old Roman Empire when Caligula, Nero and Domitian demanded worship, it was either worship the emperor or die! The same scenario will mark antichrist's rise to power, and believers will be faced with the same decision – denounce Christ and worship the "beast" (antichrist) or die! This evil emperor will go a step further to stamp out Christians as John writes in Revelation 13:16-17,

> *"He also forced everyone, small and great, rich and poor, free and slave, to receive a mark on his right hand or his forehead, so that no one could buy or sell unless he had the mark, which is the name of the beast or the number of his name."*

Just imagine not being able to purchase the necessities of life – food, clothing, shelter, and transportation! No wonder Jesus warns those in the field not even to go back to get their coats! How awful it would be for the pregnant woman or nursing mother to be on the run and not know where they will sleep or get their next meal. Even worse, Jesus says, is the followers' flight in winter when heavy rains in the area usually cause rising rivers and flooding. And if the Jewish Christian were practicing Sabbath law, this person would not be permitted to travel more than a half-mile from Friday at sundown to Saturday at sundown!

Jesus says in verse twenty-one and twenty-two,

140

"For then there will be great distress, unequaled from the beginning of the world until now – and never to be equaled again. If those days had not been cut short, no one would survive, but for the sake of the elect those days will be shortened."

Jesus is clearly speaking of the "Great Tribulation" period. This time frame is to last seven years as described by Daniel in chapter 9:25-27. This seven-year time frame is also called "Daniel's Seventieth Week."

This time of unequaled distress is also described by the prophet Daniel in Chapter 12:1a:

"At that time Michael, the great prince who protects your people, will arise. There will be a time of distress such as has not happened from the beginning of nations until then."

God's Word affirms and confirms God' Word. Scripture interprets Scripture. John, in Revelation 11:2, speaks of "Daniels Seventieth Week",

"... but exclude the outer court; do not measure it, because it has been given to the Gentiles. They will trample on the holy city for forty two months."

We see John's vision supporting Jesus' teaching: "for the sake of the elect those days will be shortened." The word "elect" simply means the people of God. This Revelation 11:2 verse demonstrates that the "Gentiles" or "pagans" will have rule over the holy city, Jerusalem, for forty-two months – three and a half years. Jesus said in Luke 21:24-26,

> *"Jerusalem will be trampled on by the Gentiles*
> *until the times of the Gentiles are fulfilled."*

The timer is already set – you and I do not know when, but we do know *Who*! Our calling is not to quibble over times and dates but to be faithful, to continue to allow His light to shine through our lives to a dark and dying generation. To the question, "When will the end come?" The answer is simple: "When the time of the Gentiles is fulfilled."

John also confirms this "shortened" time span of three and a half years in Revelation 13:5:

> *"The beast was given a mouth to utter proud*
> *words and blasphemies and to exercise his*
> *authority for forty-two months."*

John goes on to confirm the teachings of Daniel and Christ in Revelation 13:6-8:

"He opened his mouth to blaspheme God, and
to slander his name and his dwelling place
and those who live in heaven. He was given
power to make war against the saints and to
conquer them. And he was given authority
over every tribe, people, language and nation.
All inhabitants of the earth will worship the
beast, all whose names have not been written
in the Book of Life belonging to the Lamb that
was slain from the creation of the world."

No wonder Jesus described this time period as an "unparalleled and unequalled time of distress." Praise God that it will be shortened for the sake of His people. During this brief period the antichrist is going to be given authority, allowed by God to blaspheme, slander, make war against the saints, and exercise authority over all peoples and nations. To what end? Why will the antichrist do all these things? The answer is in verse eight:

"All inhabitants of the earth will worship the
beast, all whose names have not been written
in the Book of Life belonging to the Lamb..."

The "beast" (antichrist) is going to demand worship from all who live upon the earth. All unbelievers will bow down! However, the "saints," or those who have their names written in the Lamb's Book of Life – WILL NOT!

> *"He who has an ear, let him hear what the Spirit says to the churches"* (Revelation 3:22).

CHAPTER 7

LIKE LIGHTNING FROM THE EAST

(MATTHEW 24:23-51)

In the Gospel of John 14:1-6, Jesus comforts the disciples with these words,

"Do not let your hearts be troubled. Trust in God; trust also in me. In my Father's house are many rooms; if it were not so, I would have told you. I am going there to prepare a place for you. And if I go and prepare a place for you, I will come back and take you to be with me that you also may be where I am. You know the way to the place where I am going. Thomas said to him, 'Lord, we don't know where you are going, so how can we know the way?' Jesus answered, I am the way, and the

truth and the life. No one comes to the Father
except through me."

Prior to this instruction, Jesus has already told the disciples of his leaving through his death, resurrection and ascension. It is a very poignant scene as Jesus and the disciples are enjoying their last Passover meal together. In verse one Jesus encourages them,

"Do not let your hearts be troubled. Trust in
God; trust also in me."

In our study of "end time" events we must follow the instruction of Christ. Be encouraged! Trust in the Father; trust in the Son; trust in the Holy Spirit. As Paul says in 1 Thessalonians 4:18,

"Therefore encourage each other with these
words."

No matter what Satan may bring against God's true people, our Lord will take care of us and see us through.

In verse two, Jesus speaks of his Father's house:

"In my Father's house are many rooms ... I am
going there to prepare a place for you".

The word rooms in the Greek literally means "permanent dwelling places." Therefore, what Jesus is teaching is that he has returned to his Father's right hand of authority and has prepared a permanent dwelling place for all who believe in him.

Verse three is vital as well,

> *"And if I go and prepare a place for you, I will come back and take you to be with me that you also may be where I am."*

The facts are these: Jesus is leaving but only temporarily; he has prepared our dwelling place; it's with Him; we will be where he is as he will come back to take all believers to be with him in this wonderful, awesome dwelling place – which is permanent, eternal.

In verse four where Jesus says, *"You know the way to the place where I am going,"* Thomas responds openly and honestly in verse five,

> *"Lord, we don't know where you are going, so how can we know the way?" Jesus replies in verse six with the most comforting words we will ever hear,*

> *"I am the way and the truth and the life. No one comes to the Father except through me."*

In this passage – John 14:1-6, we recognize that Jesus is speaking of his Second Coming. Particularly in verse three where Christ promises to "... come back and take you with me that you also may be where I am." This is not usually associated with biblical teachings concerning "end times" events. Yet, there it is, clearly speaking of the fact that Jesus Christ is going to return. Not only is he going to return, but he is going to take his followers to be where he is. This truth from John's Gospel is a perfect backdrop to our next passage in Matthew twenty-four.

This Matthew 24:23-31 passage is to be understood as the description of Christ's coming. Jesus is speaking another warning in verses 23-26,

> *"At this time if anyone says to you, 'Look, here is the Christ!' or 'There he is!' do not believe it. For false christs and false prophets will appear and perform great signs and miracles to deceive even the elect if that were possible. See, I have told you ahead of time. So if anyone tells you, there he is, out in the desert, do no go out; or here he is in the inner rooms, do not believe it."*

This is Christ's fifth warning in twenty-six verses: "Watch out that no one deceives you" (24:4); "But see to it that you are not alarmed" (24:6); "let the reader understand" (24:15); "great distress ... never to be equaled again" (24:21); "do not believe it" (24:23 & 26)! Just as Jesus taught in verse eight about "the beginning of birth pains," in verses 9-14 we see the contractions starting to intensify.

In verse fifteen, the abomination that causes desolation. The contractions are coming closer together with the description of these events following in verses 16-22. Then, as we see in verses 23-26, Satan, through the "antichrist" and "false prophet", makes his last great attempt to deceive God's people, the elect, by not only sending false prophets, but sending *the* false prophet of Revelation 13:13,

> *"...he performed great and miraculous signs,*
> *even causing fire to come down from heaven*
> *to earth in full view of men."*

This is exactly what Jesus says in Matthew 24:24:

> *"For false christs and false prophets will*
> *appear and perform great signs and miracles*
> *to deceive even the elect – if that were*
> *possible."*

Satan's plan has always been to deceive the inhabitants of earth (Revelation 13:14). The good news is that he will not be able to deceive the elect – God's true followers – nor to keep them from seeing the true Son of God!

Just as things seem ready to shatter completely – the holy city of Jerusalem is trampled by pagans for forty-two months, believers are put to death, persecution wreaks havoc, the mark of the "beast" is enforced, the temple is taken over and used by the antichrist for false worship – finally the days of the Gentiles are fulfilled (Luke 21:24) and God's purposes are completed.

Jesus teaches in Matthew 24:27-31,

> *"For as lightning that comes from the east is visible even in the west, so will be the coming of the Son of Man. Wherever there is a carcass, there the vultures will gather. Immediately after the distress of those days, the sun will be darkened, and the moon will not give its light; the stars will fall from the sky, and the heavenly bodies will be shaken. At that time the sign of the Son of Man will appear in the sky, and all the nations of the earth will mourn. They will see the Son of Man coming on the clouds of the sky, with power and great glory. And he will send his angels with a loud trumpet call, and they will gather his elect from the four winds, from one end of the heavens to the other."*

In verse twenty-seven, we see clearly that Jesus' Coming is going to be as visible as lightning crossing a dark sky. Christ says in verse twenty-eight that his Coming will be as obvious as "vultures circling a carcass." When you or I see the vultures gathering, we know there is a dead animal close by. In verse twenty nine it reads:

"Immediately after the distress of those days..."

What distress? The great, unequalled distress of verse twenty-one,

> *"For then there will be great distress, unequalled from the beginning of the world until now – and never to be equaled again."*

What caused the "great distress"? The abomination of Matthew 24:15 and Daniel 9:27? Who is this abomination? It is the beast of Revelation 13:5-7:

> *"The beast was given a mouth to utter proud words and blasphemies and to exercise his authority for forth-two months. He opened his mouth to blaspheme God, and to slander his name and his dwelling place and those who live in heaven. He was given power to make war against the saints and to conquer them. And he was given authority over every tribe, people, language, and nation."*

Daniel speaks of this beast, or horn, in Daniel 7:21, "As I watched, this horn was waging war against the saints and defeating them." Then in Daniel 7:25, "He will speak against the Most High and oppress his saints and try to change the set times and the laws. The saints will be handed over to him for a time, times and a half" (a year, two years and half a year[1]).

Consider the phrase in Matthew 24:29:

> "Immediately after the distress of those days..."

(after all of the signs that Jesus has described in verses 4-14 and verses 15-26). Notice Christ's words are "immediately after the distress" – NOT "before the distress!" The sign of his Coming is going to take place after the great and awful persecution of the saints by the "beast" or "antichrist". Still in Matthew 24:29 we see the first sign of Jesus Christ's return:

> "Immediately after the distress of those days –
> the sun will be darkened, and the moon will
> not give its light; the stars will fall from the
> sky and the heavenly bodies will be shaken."

Did you ever wonder how the entire population of planet earth will see Christ coming? It is going to be totally dark! It should be no wonder to us, the students of his Word, that Jesus would use the analogy of lightning in verse twenty-seven! Most everyone has been involved in a bad thunderstorm when the sky is pitch black and brewing ... the storm is coming ... then all of a sudden – the light show! Lightning flies across the deep black sky and lights up the land in an instant. Listen to Jesus' words in verse thirty,

"At that time the sign of the Son of Man will appear in the sky and all the nations of the earth will mourn. They will see the Son of Man coming on the clouds of the sky, with power and great glory."

We can clearly see this scene unfolding – everything is dark – no light from the sun, no light from the moon – the stars falling from the sky and the heavenly bodies shaking! You probably have witnessed a meteor shower or a lone shooting star, a sunrise or a sunset, but no one at anytime in human history has witnessed anything like this! Against the backdrop of a "black hole" of total and complete darkness, the Son of Man – Jesus Christ – is going to appear with power and great glory! Isaiah predicted almost seven hundred years before Christ's first coming the following in Isaiah 13:9-11,

"See, the day of the Lord is coming, a cruel day, with wrath and fierce anger – to make the land desolate and destroy the sinners within it. The stars of heaven and their constellations will not show their light. The rising sun will be darkened and the moon will not give its light. I will punish the world for its evil, the wicked for their sins. I will put an end to the arrogance of the haughty and will humble the pride of the ruthless."

Isaiah further confirms Jesus' Matthew 24 teaching in Isaiah 34:4,

> *"All the stars of the heavens will be dissolved and the sky rolled up like a scroll; all the starry host will fall like withered leaves from the vine, like shriveled figs from the fig tree."*

Still in Matthew 24:30, with everyone on the planet standing in total darkness, the sign of the Son of Man appears. One group of people is about to "lift their heads for their redemption draws nigh" (Luke 21:28). The other group, "the nations of the earth, will mourn." John confirms this truth in Revelation 6:12-17,

> *"I watched as he* (the Lamb of Revelation 6:1) *opened the sixth seal. There was a great earthquake. The sun turned black like sackcloth made of goat hair; the whole moon turned blood red; and the stars in the sky fell to earth, as late figs drop from a fig tree when shaken by a strong wind. The sky receded like a scroll, rolling up, and every mountain and island was removed from its place. Then the kings of the earth, the princes, the generals, the rich, the mighty and every slave and every free man hid in caves and among the rocks of*

the mountain. They called to the mountains
and the rocks, 'Fall on us and hide us from the
face of him who sits on the throne and from
the wrath of the Lamb! For the great day of
their wrath has come and who can stand?'"

The Lord spoke through Isaiah about "humbling the pride of the ruthless" and He reveals to John what "the day of the Lord" looks like when "all the nations will mourn" at the appearance of the Son of Man – the Lamb – Jesus Christ. We go to Isaiah 24:21-23 for confirmation:

"In that day, the Lord will punish the powers
in the heavens above and the kings on the
earth below. They will be herded together like
prisoners bound in a dungeon; they will be
shut up in prison and be punished after many
days. The moon will be abashed, the sun
ashamed; for the Lord Almighty will reign on
Mount Zion and in Jerusalem, and before its
elders, gloriously."

The Lord speaks through Isaiah in verse twenty-one that He will punish Satan and all of the fallen angels (demons), "In that day the Lord will punish the powers in heaven above." This verse does not teach that Satan lives in heaven where God resides. The actual

155

word in Hebrew is translated "heavens," a plural, meaning the skies over earth. Paul confirms this in Ephesians 6:11-12,

"Put on the full armor of God so that you can take your stand against the devil's schemes. For our struggle is not against flesh and blood, but against the rulers, against the authorities, against the powers of the dark world and against the spiritual forces of evil in the heavenly realms."

We have already discussed God's punishment on "the kings of the earth below" in our Revelation 6:15-17 passage. But keep in mind God's judgment is going to be poured out on all evil and all who choose to go the path of evil. Isaiah 24:21 teaches that the punishment will be against Satan, his demonic forces, and all who reject God's plan for salvation.

In verse twenty-two we read,

"...they will be herded together like prisoners bound in a dungeon; they will be shut up in prison and be punished after many days."

John, in Revelation 20:1-2, sees

"an angel coming down out of heaven, having the key to the abyss and holding in his hand a

great chain. He seized the dragon, that
ancient serpent, who is the devil, or Satan, and
bound him for a thousand years."

God has had his people, his prophets, his teachers, and his preachers deliver the Word to the inhabitants of the earth so people of all "tribes, nations and languages" would repent of their sin and accept His plan – as revealed in and through Jesus Christ! God's word is true. Satan, who is loose on the earth still today, will not be loose much longer! He and all those who follow him will be judged and punished for their rebellion against the Great and Awesome God. Revelation 20:10 says,

"And the devil, who deceived them, was
thrown into the lake of burning sulfur, where
the beast and the false prophet had been
thrown. They will be tormented day and night
forever and ever."

The signs that open the "Great Terrible Day" of our Lord, as Jesus teaches in Matthew 24, appear again in Isaiah 24:23,

"The moon will be abashed, the sun ashamed;
for the Lord Almighty will reign on Mount
Zion and in Jerusalem, and before its elders,
gloriously."

157

The writer of Hebrews, confirming faith in God, says,

> *"But you have come to Mount Zion, to the heavenly city of Jerusalem, the city of the living God. You have come to thousands upon thousands of angels in joyful assembly, to the church of the firstborn, whose names are written in heaven. You have come to God, the judge of all men, to the spirits of righteous men made perfect, to Jesus the mediator of a new covenant and to the sprinkled blood that speaks a better word than the blood of Abel"* (Hebrews 12:22-24).

Isaiah and the writer of Hebrews are looking to the "day" when the Lord will rule from His "heavenly" city of Jerusalem. John in Revelation 22:5 affirms Isaiah 24:23,

> *"There will be no more night. They will not need the light of a lamp or the light of the sun, for the Lord God will give them light. And they will reign forever and ever."*

John elaborates in Revelation 21:23,

*"The city does not need the sun or the moon to
shine on it, for the glory of God gives it light,
and the Lamb is its lamp."*

This same Lamb who lights up the heavenly city of Jerusalem
will also light up the darkened sky of earth with His glorious
appearing! This same Lamb who is faithful and true will come for his
people "immediately *after* the "great distress" brought on by
"antichrist." Through these scripture passages we see that God does
not allow the beast to have authority but for a short time (three and
half years). We also see that God takes care of all righteous judgment
to be executed over Satan and all who reject God's salvation.

Now I want us to turn our full attention to Matthew 24:31,

*"(1) Immediately after the distress; (2) The
sun and moon are darkened; (3) stars are
falling from the sky; (4) the sign of the Son of
Man will appear in the dark hole of the sky;
(5) all nations of the earth will mourn; (6)
Everyone witnesses the coming of the Son of
Man on the clouds of the sky, with power and
great glory"* (Matthew 24:29-30).

All of this action opens the "Great Terrible Day of the Lord!"
The time for God's judgment has come. The question that needs to

be asked is: where are God's true believers – the elect – the church – the saints? The answer is in verse thirty-one:

> *"And He (the son of Man) will send his angels with a loud trumpet call, and they will gather his elect from the four winds, from one end of the heavens to the other."*

What a glorious moment in the history of the church! This is the long awaited and anticipated point in our lives when we are gathered to Christ and see Him face to face! Paul confirms this truth in 1 Thessalonians 4:16-17,

> *"For the Lord himself will come down from heaven, with a loud command, with the voice of the archangel and with the trumpet call of God, and the dead in Christ will rise first. After that, we who are still alive and are left will be caught up together with them in the clouds to meet the Lord in the air. And so we will be with the Lord forever."*

Jesus taught clearly that those who are his true followers will go through trials, tribulations, and be persecuted by "antichrist" (Matthew 24:9-13). However, true believers will NOT be on planet earth when God's judgment comes upon those who have rejected the Son of Man.

Paul comforts believers in 1 Corinthians 15:51-52,

> *"Listen, I tell you a mystery; we will not all sleep, but we will be changed – in a flash, in the twinkling of an eye, at the last trumpet. For the trumpet will sound, the dead will be raised imperishable and we will be changed."*

These two passages clearly support Jesus' teaching in Matthew 24:31. Paul obviously teaches that the Lord himself is to come down from heaven. When? At the "loud trumpet call." Jesus raises the "dead in Christ" first. Just think – all of the believers who ever lived and died will receive their resurrection body first. Then, those believers who are still alive at His coming will be changed "in the twinkling of an eye." In other words, they will receive their resurrected bodies when the Lord comes to "gather them from the four winds of heaven." Paul goes on to teach in the 1 Thessalonians 4:16-17 passage that believers (both dead and alive) will

> *"be caught up together in the clouds to meet the Lord in the air. And so will be with the Lord forever."*

This verse is the only clear New Testament reference to a "rapture" which is Latin for "snatching up" or "catching away." However, this passage, beyond any shadow of doubt, confirms Jesus' teaching of the "gathering of the elect." One can clearly see that the one and same event is being discussed.

One other note here, is that Paul undeniably states: "we will be with the Lord forever." This one phrase helps the reader to understand that when Christ gathers his elect from the sinful world, they will not be sent back or cast out, or neglected – they will "be with the Lord forever." Just as Jesus taught in the John 14:1-6 passage,

> *"He has gone to prepare a permanent place*
> *for his followers to live with Him forever!"*

This is a wonderful encouraging word for us today. Even as we bear our own trials, tribulations, persecutions and sorrows, we know that our God is going to deliver us from all of the struggles of this fallen nature. His word does not, has not and will not ever teach that His followers will never experience problems. Quite the contrary. Paul speaks to this in Romans 8:35-39,

> *"Who shall separate us from the love of*
> *Christ? Shall trouble or hardship or*
> *persecution or famine or nakedness or danger*
> *or sword? As it is written: 'For your sake we*
> *face death all day long; we are considered as*
> *sheep to be slaughtered'. No, in all these things*
> *we are more than conquerors through him*

who loved us. For I am convinced that neither death nor life, neither angels nor demons, neither the present nor the future, nor any powers, neither height nor depth, nor anything else in all creation, will be able to separate us from the love of God that is in Christ Jesus our Lord."

Look at the phrase "nor anything in all creation." Satan, the "antichrist," the false prophet, and the demons are ALL created beings! Yet they cannot separate the true child of God from the "love of God in Jesus Christ!"

I encourage you to study the life of the Apostle Paul. You will quickly understand this Romans 8:35-39 passage, as Paul, throughout his service to Christ, was beaten, shipwrecked, persecuted, jailed, faced troubles, hardships, rejection and finally died a martyr's death! Why would he face all of these? Because of his love for his risen Savior! How can we face the hardships of our lives? Rejection? Persecution? Physical death? We know nothing can separate us from Christ's love. Therefore, we can face anything. Philippians 4:13 leaps to mind. Here Paul writes,

"I can do all things through Christ who gives me strength."

We do not and will not have to face any opposition alone! Jesus said in Matthew 28:20b as He is issuing the Great Commission,

> *"And surely I am with you always, to the very end of the age."*

Our God repeatedly promised Moses, Joshua and the children of Israel,

> *"Be strong and courageous. Do not be afraid or terrified because of them (enemies), for the Lord your God goes with you; he will never leave you nor forsake you"* (Deuteronomy 31:6).

God speaks to Abraham in a vision in Genesis 15:1,

> *"Do not be afraid, Abram. I am your shield, your very great reward."*

What God is saying to all "believers" is no matter what this life may bring – I am your shield, your sovereign, your king, and your protector. I am your very great reward! The Lord spoke this comfort to His people of days past. He speaks comfort to us today and He speaks words of comfort to those who will faithfully follow in the future. No matter what persecution or "great distress" is brought on God's people by the "antichrist" or the "beast" – Our Lord will see us through! He is truly the only One who will never leave us nor forsake us!

The Fig Tree

Let us now examine the next passage in Matthew 24. Jesus continues teaching concerning the signs of the end of the age. In verses 32-35, Christ speaks,

> *"Now learn this lesson from the fig tree: As soon as its twigs get tender and its leaves come out, you know that summer is near. Even so, when you see all these things, you know that it (He) is near, right at the door. I tell you the truth, this generation will certainly not pass away until all these things have happened. Heaven and earth will pass away, but my words will never pass away."*

What importance or significance does the "lesson from the fig tree" hold? Why and what does Jesus want us to learn from it? Let's look to Luke's Gospel where Jesus is teaching a parable concerning a fig tree. Luke 13:6-9,

> *"Then he told this parable: 'A man had a fig tree, planted in his vineyard, and he went to look for fruit on it, but did not find any. So he*

165

said to the man who took care of the vineyard,
'For three years now I've been coming to look
for fruit on this fig tree and haven't found any.
Cut it down! Why should it use up the soil?
'Sir,' the man replied, 'leave it alone for one
more year, and I'll dig around it and fertilize
it. If it bears fruit next year, fine! If not, then
cut it down.'"

Jesus, in several parables, used grapevines and fig trees as a symbol of the nation of Israel. The reference in this passage of the fig tree is the nation of Israel. In this parable in Luke, Jesus is teaching about finding no fruit ("spiritual fruit," or faith) in the house of Israel, particularly in its rulers.

Through the prophet Hosea, God speaks of Israel,

"When I found Israel, it was like finding
grapes in the desert; when I saw your fathers,
it was like seeing the early fruit on the fig tree
(Hosea 9:10a)."

God is speaking of his love for Israel and his heart-felt desire for intimate fellowship with his people. For this to occur, God's true people must be willing to obey. Because of their disobedience and rejection of Messiah, judgment must come. In the Gospel of Mark, we come upon this scene:

"The next day as they were leaving for Bethany, Jesus was hungry. Seeing in the distance a fig tree in leaf, he went to find out if it had any fruit. When he reached it, he found nothing but leaves, because it was not the season for figs. Then he said to the tree, 'May no one ever eat fruit from you again.' And his disciples heard him say it ... In the morning, as they went along, they saw the fig tree withered from its roots (Mark 11:12-14, 20)."

This Mark passage sheds light on the Luke parable – that God is looking for spiritual fruit in the fig tree or nation of Israel. Because He found none, judgment is to come on the house of Israel. John the Baptizer, in Matthew 3:10, said of the coming judgment,

"The ax is already at the root of the trees and every tree that does not produce good fruit will be cut down and thrown in the fire."

Because of the nation of Israel's (the chief priests' and Pharisees') rejection of the Messiah, Jesus Christ, judgment was coming. In Matthew 21:42-43 Jesus quotes Psalm 118:22-23,

"have you never read in the Scriptures: 'The stone the builders rejected has become the capstone; the Lord has done this, and it is

marvelous in our eyes.' Therefore, I tell you
that the kingdom of God will be taken away
from you and given to a people who will
produce its fruit."

Jesus, speaking of producing fruit, says in John 15:5-8,

"I am the vine; you are the branches. If a man
remains in me and I in him, he will bear much
fruit; apart from me you can do nothing. If
anyone does not remain in me, his is like a
branch that is thrown into the fire and
burned. If you remain in me and my words
remain in you, ask whatever you wish, and it
will be given you. This is to my Father's glory,
that you bear much fruit showing yourselves
to be my disciples."

How does all this teaching of the "fig tree" relate to the fig tree in Matthew 24:32? The fig tree in this verse is the nation of Israel. We have already discussed the partial judgment that came on Israel for rejecting Christ, namely the Roman siege of Jerusalem and subsequent destruction of the Jewish temple in 70 AD: "The 'Diaspora' began about this time with the dispersal of Jews living in and around Palestine. With the fall of the temple, Judaism took a major blow and was strongly influenced by Greek and Roman thought and philosophy. Thus, with no temple or center of worship, many Jews with no "homeland" to call their own, began to migrate to other parts of the world."[2] There was no nation of Israel for almost nineteen centuries! Jesus says,

> *"As soon as its twigs get tender and its leaves*
> *come out, you will know that summer is near*
> *(Matthew 24:32)."*

The "twigs" were not possible since the Roman destruction of the first century. That is, until 1948 when Israel received her statehood and was recognized by the world community as a nation once more. Not surprisingly, God spoke of this restoration through the prophet Zephaniah,

> *"At that time I will gather you; at that time I*
> *will bring you home. I will give you honor and*
> *praise among all the peoples of the earth*
> *when I bring back your captives before your*
> *very eyes. (Zephaniah 3:20)."*

This prophecy is to be understood as to the true remnant of the true people of God – those Jews who will receive Messiah during the tribulation period. Therefore, God gathered this nation of Israel in 1948 as the beginning phase of the final restoration of Jerusalem under Messiah's reign.

In 1948, with statehood restored, we see "the twigs getting tender." Yet Israel still had no control over her beloved city of Jerusalem. That is, until 1967, when Israel defeated a coalition of Arab States (Egypt, Syria, Jordan, Saudi Arabia) and regained Jerusalem, her capitol city, in the Six-Days War. With this event the twigs are not just tender – "the leaves are coming out." Summer is near. In verse thirty-three, Jesus says,

> "Even so, when you see all of these things, you
> know that it (he) is near, right at the door."

The Greek word for "it" can also be translated as "he". Thus, "he," the Son of Man, is near. He is right at the door.

In verse thirty-four, Jesus says,

> "I tell you the truth, this generation (race) will
> certainly not pass away until all these things
> have happened."

The Greek word used here for "generation" can also be translated "race," as in a race or nationality of people. Either way, the word Jesus used means a group of people. What people? Look at the text,

> "This generation (race) will certainly not pass
> away until all these things have happened."

The people Jesus is speaking of is the group that sees the "twigs getting tender" and "the leaves coming out." This group of people "will certainly not pass until all these things have happened" (Matthew 24:34). Summer is near when we see the fig tree's twigs getting tender (Israel becoming a nation in 1948) – and it's leaves coming out – getting closer (1967 regaining Jerusalem). The group of people who witness the beginning of the lesson from the fig tree "will not pass until all of these things have happened."

Christ closes out this passage with a vivid reminder,

> *"Heaven and earth will pass away, but my words will never pass away."*

We know from Revelation 21:1a that there will be a new heaven and a new earth. Jesus writes,

> *"Then I saw a new heaven and a new earth, for the first heaven and the first earth had passed away."*

Creation under the curse of sin is going to be "made new" by its Creator. His words will never pass away. This truth can only be spoken of our God. He is the only one we can fully count on and trust. Also, Jesus is teaching his followers that his prophecy is true and will come to pass just as He has said. We can trust Him and the words he speaks for they bring life. In the Gospel of John, the Apostle John speaks of Jesus in John 1:3-4,

"Through him all things were made; without him nothing was made that has been made. In Him was life, and that life was the light of men."

Allow Him to be your light today. Jesus Christ is the only one who can shed light/truth on His prophecies. Ask the Holy Spirit to reveal to you the truth He desires you to know.

The Significance of 1948

1948 was a very significant year in terms of bible prophecy, particularly "end time" events. As we have already recounted, Israel regained statehood. This one piece in the prophetic puzzle had to take place to set up Daniel 9:27, where the "beast" (antichrist) forbids the Jews to worship in their rebuilt temple in Jerusalem. Obviously, the 1967 event of Israel regaining Jerusalem is vital as well. However, I want to focus our attention on several crucial events that occurred in 1948.

World War II had finally ended in victory by the Allies, but certainly not without a tremendous cost. Europe was in chaos and devastation was seemingly everywhere as much of the fighting had taken place on her soil. There was a call by some for unification of Europe so as to not allow the horrors of war to take place again in their homelands. Also, a United Europe could economically compete with the United States and the Soviet Union as a world power. "This call for a united Europe started in 1948 and began in earnest in 1957 as the European Economic Community at a treaty signing in Rome."[1] This "revived Roman Empire" is spoken of by the prophet Daniel in chapter 7:23-24a ...

> *"The fourth beast is a fourth kingdom that will appear on earth. It will be different from the other kingdoms and will devour the whole earth... the ten horns are ten kings who will come from this kingdom."*

The antichrist will arise from this revised kingdom (Daniel 7:25) only to be defeated by the Most High (7:27). Rome is to be the capitol of this "Revised Roman Empire" (Revelation 17:9, 18).

"The EEC started with only six members (France, West Germany, the Netherlands, Belgium, Luxembourg, Italy), with the goal of having ten. As stated in a Time magazine article in 1979, "Should all go according to the most optimistic schedules, the 'Common Market' could someday expand into a 10-nation economic entity."[2] Even as far back as 1948, these six original members called themselves the "Big Ten." Even their currency is prophetic as on the back of a Euro coin is a woman riding a beast (right out of Revelation 17).

Another important event took place in 1948, the formation of the World Council of Churches. This agreement paves the way for the false prophet to have a power base from which to speak. This group's original intent may have been for good. However, it is most difficult today to see any spiritual fruit (Galatians 5:22-23 – love, joy, peace, longsuffering, kindness, goodness, faithfulness, gentleness, self control) coming out of this organization at all. Most of their agenda is politically motivated – NOT spiritual at all. This will play right into the hands of the beast (antichrist) and his false prophet (Revelation 13).

Lastly, a most important invention took place in 1948: the creation of the transistor. This tiny electronic device has opened the technological door for a myriad of electronic inventions, including our present-day computer. On the Internet we can communicate with people across the globe instantly. We can purchase, sell or trade goods within seconds. With the ability of computer technology, the antichrist will be able to "monitor" the world's population by the use of satellites. This is already happening as human beings are presently being tracked all over the world.

All of these events of 1948 are lining up just as our God, through His Son, the prophets, and the apostles, predicted. Current events are also beginning to fit perfectly into the prophetic puzzle. Thus, the stage is being set for Daniel's seventieth week, the coming of antichrist and the false prophet. More importantly, though, God continues to place the pieces of His "end time" puzzle to prepare for the coming of the Son of Man – Jesus Christ.

* Thanks to John Courson and Searchlight Ministries, for some facts shared in this section.

The Olivet Discourse

Matthew 24:1 through Matthew 25:46 is the fifth and final of Christ's teachings known as the Olivet discourse. There are three major parables taught by Jesus in Matthew twenty-five. Yet, I want to focus our attention on the final three passages of chapter twenty-four that further illuminate our Savior's teaching about the signs of His coming and the end of the age.

In verses thirty-six through forty-one, Jesus says,

> *"No one knows about that day or hour, not even the angels in heaven, nor the son, but only the Father. As it was in the days of Noah, so it will be at the coming of the Son of Man. For in the days before the flood, people were eating and drinking, marrying and giving in marriage, up to the day Noah entered the ark; and they knew nothing about what would happen until the flood came and took them all away. That is how it will be at the coming of the Son of Man. Two men will be in the field; one will be taken and the other left. Two women will be grinding with a hand mill; one will be taken and the other left."*

In verse thirty-six, Jesus shares a truth that no one knows the hour of his "*parousia*" or his coming except the Father. The timetable is already set from eternity past. The angels do not need to know; human beings do not need to know. We need to be faithful. "He who stands firm to the end will be saved" (Matthew 24:13).

Some manuscripts do not have, *nor the Son,* in this verse. No matter. It is not important whether Jesus knew the "day and hour" of his coming while in his earthly body. He knows NOW. As the second person of the Trinity – trust me – He knows NOW!

Jesus gives the example of Noah in verses thirty-seven through thirty-nine. At his coming, life will be going on as it "was in the days of Noah." For people were *"eating, drinking, marrying and giving in marriage"* – going about their lives not paying any attention to the Creator nor his messenger – living life their way. Noah preached for about one hundred years, and outside of his wife, three sons, and their wives, no one believed (2 Peter 2:5, Hebrews 11:7). Noah responded to God by faith, taking on the seemingly overwhelming task of building a 450 ft. long, 75 ft. wide, and 45 ft. high, sea-worthy vessel (Genesis 6:15). Not only did Noah build the ark – he built it inland in a landlocked area where it was unthinkable that there would ever be enough water to float it! Noah obviously responded to God by faith and obedience. Jesus is teaching in this passage that all those who do likewise (respond to God by faith) will be saved from the judgment of God on the Terrible Day of the Lord.

Jesus says that the people of Noah's day were "eating drinking, marrying and giving in marriage, up to the day Noah entered the ark." Look at each of these activities – all were seemingly good things to do. Yet, these people were rebellious, choosing to live their lives their own way – WITHOUT GOD! The finality of their lives and activities came when Noah entered the ark. In verse thirty-nine it says,

> "...they knew nothing about what would happen until the flood came and took them all away."

Why didn't they know? Noah had told them about the coming judgment. They did not know because they chose NOT TO BELIEVE.

> "That is how it will be at the coming of the Son of Man" (verse 39:b). "Two men in the field; one will be taken and the other left. Two women will be grinding with a hand mill; one will be taken and the other left" (verses 40-46).

Keep this reference to Jesus' teaching of 24:31:
... and he (Son of Man) will send his angels with a loud trumpet call, and they will gather his elect from the four winds, from one end of the heavens to the other."
This example of "one taken and one left" is a description of how the "rapture" (gathering of the elect) will be. This is not, as some have portrayed, a "secret gathering." Jesus clearly said earlier,

"... all the nations will mourn. They will see the Son of Man coming on the clouds of the sky, with power and glory."

On this awesome day the believer will be taken to meet Jesus in the air and the unbeliever will be left to face "the wrath of the Lamb" (Revelation 6:16b).

"Therefore keep watch, because you do not know on what day your Lord will come. But understand this: If the owner of the house had known at what time of night the thief was coming, he would have kept watch and would not have let his house be broken into. So you also must be ready, because the Son of Man will come at an hour when you do not expect him" (Matthew 24: 42-44).

The truths found in verses 36-41 cause Jesus to issue another warning in verse forty-two,

"Therefore keep watch because you do not know on what day your Lord will come."

I have already mentioned how knowing the exact day and hour of Christ's return would be a hindrance to true faith. Knowing would not help true believers at all, no more than knowing the hour and day of our death. Yet, Jesus has given us plenty of signs in His word through His own teachings, through the prophets and apostles that help us understand as this awesome event draws near. The key phrase in verse forty-two is, "therefore keep watch." Therefore – meaning – based on the previous information concerning the signs of His return – the believer needs to be ready at every moment. The spiritual truth is this – human beings need to have their relationship with Christ right whether one would face physical death before his return or be alive at his coming. We must be ready to meet Him.

"Keep watch" does not mean for us to get our white robes on and do nothing as if we were sitting at the bus stop waiting for the bus. What it does mean, as Jesus explains in verse forty-three and following,

> *"But understand this: If the owner of the house had known at what time of night the thief was coming, he would have kept watch and would not have let his house be broken into."*

The phrase "at what time of night" does not mean the exact moment; it means that if the owner was ready and prepared at any given moment he could have thwarted the thief's intention of breaking in the owner's house. Verse forty-four now makes more sense,

"So you also must be ready, because the Son of
Man will come at an hour when you do not
expect him."

We must be ready for His coming by being in right relationship to Christ. Paul reminds believers in 1 Thessalonians 5:6,

"So then, let us not be like the others, who are
asleep, but let us be alert and self controlled."

Paul uses the phrase "be alert;" Jesus uses the term "watch." They mean the same thing.

Christ gives a contrast of spiritual readiness in verses forty-five through fifty-one: He begins with a question,

"Who then is the faithful and wise servant
whom the master has put in charge of the
servants in his household to give them their
food at the proper time? It will be good for
that servant whose master finds doing so
when he returns. I tell you the truth, he will
put him in charge of all his possessions."

This portion of the passage is the positive side of the contrast. In this parable, the master is Christ, the servant represents the believers, and the assignment of giving food at the proper time represents our calling as Christians to be faithful to Jesus while he is away.

In verse forty-six, *"It will be good for that servant whose master finds him doing so when he returns."* Jesus is speaking of the servant being faithful to finish all tasks given him by the master. Jesus confirms this faithfulness or readiness in Revelation 16:15a,

> *"Behold, I come like a thief! Blessed is he who stays awake."* Christ goes on to speak of *"how good it will be for the faithful servant, as the master will put him in charge of all his possessions"* (verse forty-seven).

Jesus confirms this truth of the faithful servant twice in the parable of the talents in Matthew 25:21,23,

> *"His master replied, "Well done, good and faithful servant! You have been faithful with a few things; I will put you in charge of many things. Come and share your master's happiness!"*

That is a great depiction of our God. He desires, even requires, our faithfulness and obedience, which in turn allows Him the freedom to pour out his full and rich blessings on His faithful and obedient children.

But there is an alternate path and result as well. In verses forty-eight through fifty-one,

> *"But suppose that servant is wicked and says to himself 'My master is staying away a long time,' and he begins to beat his fellow servants and to eat and drink with drunkards. The master of that servant will come on a day when he does not expect him and at an hour he is not aware of. He will cut him to pieces and assign him a place with the hypocrites, where there will be weeping and gnashing of teeth."*

This servant is wicked; he proves this by willfully disobeying and rebelling against the master – Christ. This servant made a very bad choice when he said to himself, "My master is staying away a long time." Sin so often begins with a wrong thought. His downfall began with this very poor decision. This servant in essence said, "I will be in charge of my life. I will do what I want to do." His lifestyle reflected his poor decision as he allowed himself to get lost in the pleasures of this world by eating and drinking with the ungodly. Therefore, when the master arrived, this servant was not ready, not alert, and did not watch to be prepared for the master's return. What is the result of his rebellion? He beats his fellow servants and eats and drinks with drunkards. Verse fifty-one is most chilling, saying the master *"will cut him to pieces and assign him a place with the hypocrites, where there will be weeping and gnashing of teeth."*

As we close our study of Matthew 24, I want to encourage you again to become a *Berean*. (A Berean was one who would check out all the Scriptures Paul shared in Acts 17. These people were not lazy- they would look into God's Word to see the truth from the preaching they had heard) Please check out all of the scriptures referenced in this chapter. And for further illumination of Christ's teaching in this section of the Olivet Discourse, study the three parables found in Matthew 25:1-46. Using Jesus' words to interpret Jesus' words is always the best method of understanding the Scriptures.

CHAPTER 8

THE END OF THE WORLD

(AS FORETOLD BY THE BOOK OF DANIEL)

One of the best biblical resources of teachings concerning "end time" events is the book of Daniel. In this collection of events, dreams and visions, the man Daniel receives exact and precise revelation from God. The truth Daniel received illuminates our study today. Everything the student of prophecy needs to know is supplied by our awesome Creator – much through His servant Daniel.

We open this portion of our study in chapter two of the book of Daniel. The great Babylonian king Nebuchadnezzar has had a dream that troubled him greatly. When the king is troubled that usually means trouble for those who serve the king. The situation is this - the king has had this disturbing dream and he wants to know what it means. Nebuchadnezzar calls in all of the wise men for them to give him the correct interpretation. One minor problem – the king refuses to tell them what he dreamed. The king's counselors are in a desperate situation. It is about to get worse as the king is angered –

he continues to refuse to share any details from his dream and orders all of the wise men of Babylon to be executed! This includes Daniel and all of the Hebrew exiles who were serving in the king's court.

Daniel does what any wise man would do at a time like this – he and his three friends, Shadrach, Meschach and Abednego, cry out to God. Their prayers are answered - the Lord reveals the mystery to Daniel in a vision. Daniel goes to the executioner and calls for a stay. Arioch, commander of the king's guard, immediately takes Daniel to Nebuchadnezzar. We pick the story up in verse thirty-one, with Daniel speaking to the king,

"You looked, O king, and there before you stood a large statue – an enormous, dazzling statue, awesome in appearance. The head of the statue was made of pure gold, its chest and arms of silver, its belly and thighs of bronze, its legs of iron, its feet partly of iron and partly of baked clay. While you were watching a rock was cut out, but not by human hands. It struck the statue on its feet of iron and clay and smashed them. Then the iron, the clay, the bronze, the silver and the gold were broken into pieces at the same time and became like chaff on a threshing floor in the summer. The

wind swept them away without leaving a trace. But the rock that struck the statue became a huge mountain and filled the whole earth (Daniel 2:31-35)."

Remember, Daniel not only interpreted the dream, he had to tell the king what the king had dreamed! In verses 36-38, Daniel says to Nebuchadnezzar,

"This was the dream, and now we will interpret it to the king. You, O king, are the king of kings. The God of heaven has given you dominion and power and might and glory; in your hands he has placed mankind and the beasts of the field and the birds of the air. Wherever they live, he has made you ruler over them all. You are the head of gold."

The prophet Jeremiah confirms this in Jeremiah 27:6,

"Now I will hand all your countries over to my servant Nebuchadnezzar, King of Babylon; I will make even the wild animals subject to him."

In other words, as the Lord God spoke this word through Jeremiah, nothing would be outside of Nebuchadnezzar's authority or dominion. Thus, Daniel's usage of the phrase "king of kings." This phrase is used differently by Paul in 1 Timothy 6:15 in application to Jesus' second coming,

"which God will bring about in his own time –
God, the blessed only Ruler, the King of kings
and Lord of lords."

Note the use of capital letters K, as King over all kings and L for Lord over all lords.

John, writing in Revelation 19:16 said,

"On his robe and on his thigh he has this name
written: KING OF KINGS AND LORD OF
LORDS."

This is describing Jesus upon his return from the battle of Armageddon. Thus, we witness the Sovereign God allowing Nebuchadnezzar – King of Babylon to be one of the first to rule planet earth and we see clearly that ultimately Jesus will reign over all.

But first, back to the dream. Verse thirty-nine,

"After you, another kingdom will rise, inferior
to yours."

We look back in history to see that the "silver chest and arms" represented the Medo-Persian Empire. The Babylonian empire fell in 539 B.C., as Cyrus led this overthrow and ushered in this second great kingdom.

Still in verse thirty-nine,

> *"Next, a third kingdom, one of bronze, will rule over the whole earth."*

This empire represented by the statue's "bronze belly and thighs" is that of Alexander the Great of Greece. Alexander came to power in about 330 BC.

I want to encourage you to pay close attention to Daniel's revelation concerning the Roman Empire, which came to power on the world scene in about 68 B.C. Daniel says in verses forty through forty-two,

> *"Finally, there will be a fourth kingdom, strong as iron – for iron breaks and smashes everything – and as iron breaks things to pieces, so it will crush and break all the others."* Historically this is exactly what is known of the old Roman Empire: she came and smashed all vestiges of the previous kingdoms. Why would I use the term "old"? Because we see in the rest of Daniel's

interpretation some very interesting truths. Some light is shed in verse forty-one,

> *"Just as you saw that the feet and toes were partly of baked clay and partly of iron, so this will be a divided kingdom; yet it will have some of the strength of iron in it, even as you saw iron mixed with clay."*

There is a distinction between the statue's "legs of iron" and its "feet of partly iron and partly of baked clay (verse 33)." As you see, the legs are iron and not mixed with any other elements. This represents the "old" Roman Empire, which smashed all of the kingdoms in her path.

The toes represent a mixture of peoples and kingdoms and of a different time. Let's look in verse forty-two,

> *"As the toes were partly iron and partly clay, so this kingdom will be partly strong and partly brittle."*

This description is not what is known about the "old" Roman Empire. Daniel goes on to say in verse thirty-three,

> *"And just as you saw the iron mixed with baked clay, so the people will be a mixture and*

will not remain united, any more than the iron

mixes with clay."

The "old" Roman Empire was constantly attacked by barbaric tribes, yet she always managed to crush her opposition. This kingdom eventually fell from within.

The feet and toes are connected to the legs – the iron legs – old Rome. The "feet partly of iron and partly of baked clay" – a future, revised Roman Empire. Verse forty-four gives us a clue,

"In the time of those kings, the God of heaven

will set up a kingdom that will never be

destroyed, nor will it be left to another people.

It will crush all those kingdoms and bring

them to an end, but it will itself endure

forever."

Jesus Christ's first coming was during the "old" Roman Empire. His atoning work on the cross and his resurrection defeated sin, death and hell. His kingdom was near because of his presence as the Incarnate Son of God. However, Jesus did not consummate his kingdom at that time. This consummation (or completion) as I have already alluded to, with Christ as the, "Lord of Lords and King of Kings" (1 Timothy 6:15, Revelation 19:16), will take place at His Second Coming.

In verse forty-four, it is clear to all that God has yet to establish on earth the kingdom that will never be destroyed. He will do so in the "time of these kings", who represent the "toes of iron and clay." This is clearly what the king's dream in verse thirty-four teaches.

> *"While you were watching, a rock was cut out,*
> *but not by human hands. It struck the statue*
> *on its feet of iron and clay and smashed them."*

The rock – Jesus' kingdom – is going to strike the statue during the time of the feet and toes or what's left of the Roman "connection" of the statue. Jesus begins His earthly reign after defeating all foes (see Revelation 19:11) We then see this in verse thirty-five:

> *"Then the iron, the clay, the bronze, the silver*
> *and the gold were broken to pieces at the*
> *same time and became like chaff on a*
> *threshing floor in the summer. The wind swept*
> *them away without leaving a trace. But the*
> *rock that struck the statue became a huge*
> *mountain and filled the whole earth."*

When Christ strikes the feet and toes of the statue – all of the earthly kingdoms are destroyed. The reference to chaff should teach us all about the brevity of our life here on earth. Chaff, the waste or unusable portions of grain, is like a light powder. All of these kingdoms are going to be "blown away" without leaving a trace.

These kingdoms are going to be replaced by the "rock of our salvation." This is the meaning of the vision of the "rock cut out of a mountain, but not by human hands" – a rock that broke the iron, the bronze, the clay, the silver and the gold to pieces (Daniel 2:45a).

One might ask, "Who is the rock?" I will allow God's Word through Isaiah to speak to us with the answer:

> "So this is what the Sovereign Lord says: See I lay a stone in Zion, a tested stone, a precious cornerstone for a sure foundation; the one who trusts will never be dismayed (Isaiah 28:16)." Paul also speaks of the foundation in 1 Corinthians 3:11,
>
> "For no one can lay any foundation other than the one already laid, which is Jesus Christ."

Peter adds a warning to those who choose to reject the cornerstone. In 1 Peter 2:7-8, the apostle writes,

> "Now to you who believe, this stone is precious. But to those who do not believe, 'The stone the builders rejected has become a capstone', and a stone that causes men to stumble and a rock that makes them fall."

Daniel's Dream of Four Beasts

Our next stop in the book of Daniel is in chapter seven. Here, we see Daniel's dream of four great beasts. In verses two and three, the prophet speaks,

> *"In my vision at night I looked and there before me were the four winds of heaven churning up the great sea. Four great beasts, each different from the others, came up out of the sea."*

The great sea represents the world-full of nations and peoples.

> *"The four great beasts are four great kingdoms that will rise from the earth."*
> (Daniel 7:17)

This dream of Daniel's seems to correspond to Nebuchadnezzar's dream that we have discussed from Daniel chapter two. Almighty God revealed to Daniel the king's dream and now He is revealing more of the "end time" events to the prophet. Take note of the similarities of this dream to the one of King Nebuchadnezzar.

In verse four,

"The first was like a lion, and it had the wings of an eagle. I watched until its wings were torn off and it was lifted from the ground so that it stood on two feet like a man, and the heart of a man was given it."

The first "beast" symbolizes the Neo-Babylonian Empire. The tearing off of the wings, the standing on two feet like a man and giving a man's heart to it refers to God's humbling of Nebuchadnezzar in Daniel chapter four.[1]

Verse five reads,

"And there before me was a second beast, which looked like a bear. It was raised up on one of its sides, and it had three ribs in its mouth between its teeth. I was told, 'Get up and eat your fill of flesh!"

"This beast represents the Medo-Persian Empire, with the Persians holding a superior status. The three ribs probably refer to their three biggest victories – Lydia, Babylon and Egypt".[2] Daniel lived long enough to witness this "beast" come to power.

In verse six, we read,

"After that, I looked and there before me was another beast, one that looked like a leopard. And on its back it had four wings like those of

a bird. This beast had four heads, and it was
given authority to rule."

This leopard with four wings speaks of the speed with which Alexander the Great conquered most of the known world. The four heads represent the four main divisions of his empire upon his death at age thirty-two. [3]

In verse seven, we see the last of the four kingdoms,

"After that, in my vision at night I looked and
there before me was a fourth beast –
terrifying and frightening and very powerful.
It had large iron teeth; it crushed and
devoured its victims and trampled underfoot
whatever was left. It was different from all the
former beasts and it had ten horns."

This fourth and final kingdom corresponds with the Roman Empire. Its iron teeth relate to the legs of iron in Nebuchadnezzar's dream in Daniel, chapter two. This creature's ten horns also correspond to the ten toes of the king's earlier dream.[4] A possible prophetic clue to the "end time" confederation is in the phrase "trampled underfoot whatever was left." This matches up with the "feet of iron and clay mixed."

This dream of Daniel's "beasts" aligns perfectly with John's "beast" in Revelation 13:1-2,

"And I saw a beast coming out of the sea. He had ten horns and seven heads, with ten crowns on his horns, and on each head a blasphemous name. The beast I saw resembled a leopard, but had feet like those of a bear and a mouth like that of a lion. The dragon gave the beast his power and his throne and great authority."

Satan gave the "old" Roman emperors their idea of emperor worship and he will give the "beast" or "antichrist" the same idea. The Roman emperor Domitian, who was in power when John wrote the book of Revelation, demanded to be addressed as "our lord and god." Please note that I refuse to capitalize the l in lord or the g in god. It was Satan who, in Luke 4:5-8, tempted Jesus with the same deal:

"The devil led him up to a high place and showed him in an instant all the kingdoms of the world. And he said to him, 'I will give you all their authority and splendor, for it has been given to me, and I can give it to anyone I want to. So if you worship me, it will all be yours.' Jesus answered,

'It is written: Worship the Lord your God and
serve him only.'"

What an awesome lesson for the follower of Christ today –
when the tempter comes to tempt, use the Word of God to seize the
victory:

> *"They overcame him by the blood of the Lamb*
> *and by the word of their testimony!"*
> (Revelation 12:11a).

This beast in Daniel 7:7 had ten horns just as the dragon in
Revelation 12:3,

> *"Then another sign appeared in heaven: an*
> *enormous red dragon with seven heads and*
> *ten horns and seven crowns on his heads."*

It is clear to see the Scripture is speaking of one and the same
- from the fourth kingdom of Daniel seven will come the "end time"
kingdom of "antichrist" found throughout the book of Revelation. Do
not forget that Satan gives this world leader his authority.

Daniel writes in 7:8,

> *"While I was thinking about the horns, there*
> *before me was another horn, a little one,*
> *which came up among them; and three of the*

first horns were uprooted before it. This horn
had eyes like the eyes of a man and a mouth
that spoke boastfully."

Satan has had many "horns" down through the ages – yet this "little one" is a world leader at the time of the return of Christ. Look at the description of heavenly judgment in 7:9-10, Daniel writes,

"As I looked, thrones were set in place, and the
Ancient of Days took his seat. His clothing was
as white as snow; the hair of his head was
white like wool. His throne was flaming with
fire, and its wheels were all ablaze. A river of
fire was flowing, coming out from before him.
Thousands upon thousands attended him; ten
thousand times ten thousand stood before
him. The court was seated, and the books were
opened."

This is a perfect description of Judgment Day. A companion passage is found in Revelation 20:11-15,

"Then I saw a great white throne and him who
was seated on it. Earth and sky fled from his
presence, and there was no place for them.
And I saw the dead, great and small, standing
before the throne, and books were opened.

Another book was opened, which is the Book of Life. The dead were judged according to what they had done as recorded in the books. The sea gave up the dead that were in it, and death and Hades gave up the dead that were in them, and each person was judged according to what he had done. Then death and Hades were thrown into the lake of fire. The lake of fire is the second death. If anyone's name was not found written in the Book of Life, he was thrown into the lake of fire."

Daniel 7:11 confirms this truth,

"Then I continued to watch because of the boastful words the horn was speaking. I kept looking until the beast was slain and its body destroyed and thrown into the blazing fire."

I mentioned earlier concerning the study of prophecy that there are both short-term and long-term views. God has revealed to Daniel, who is a trustworthy and faithful servant, the "beasts" or kingdoms that would dominate planet earth. One is going to rise to power out of the remains of the fourth kingdom at the close of time – God's Judgment Day.

In Revelation 19:20, the Lord confirms Daniel 7:11,

"But the beast was captured, and with him the false prophet who had performed the miraculous signs on his behalf. With these signs he had deluded those who had received the mark of the beast and worshipped his image. The two of them were thrown alive into the lake of burning sulfur."

Another key teaching I mentioned is the necessity of comparing Scripture with Scripture. When we line God's Word up with other parts of His Word – we will see the Truth. The picture of prophecy, or any subject for that matter, becomes increasingly clearer. The dreams and visions God started revealing to Daniel are completed by His divine revelation to John.

In Daniel 7:13-14, we see a most significant scene.

"In my vision at night I looked and there before me was one like the Son of Man, coming with the clouds of heaven. He approached the Ancient of Days and was led into his presence. He was given authority, glory and sovereign power: all peoples, nations and men of every language worshipped him. His dominion is an everlasting dominion that will not pass away, and his kingdom is one that will never be destroyed."

Earlier we discussed many of the facets of the messianic title "Son of Man", which Jesus most often used for Himself. In this Daniel 7:13-14 passage, we see for the first time in Scripture a reference to Messiah as the Son of Man. All of the previous earthly kingdoms have failed and fallen. This kingdom of the Son of Man – the rock that was cut out not by human hands – will be an everlasting dominion; it will not pass away nor be destroyed.

Revelation 5:12-13 says,

> *"Worthy is the Lamb, who was slain, to receive power and wealth and wisdom and strength and honor and glory and praise! Then I heard every creature in heaven and on earth and under the earth and on the sea, and all that is in them singing: To him who sits on the throne and to the Lamb be praise and honor and glory and power forever and ever!"*

Also, in Daniel 7:14 we see *"all peoples, nations and men of every language worshipped him."* Two things come to mind. One is the story of the tower of Babel from Genesis 11. Man's sin caused him to be "divided, have confused languages and scattered over the face of the whole earth (Genesis 11:8-9). Jesus Christ, the Lamb of God re-unites mankind as "men of every language come together to worship Him!"

In Daniel 7:17, we see confirmation of our discussion of the four beasts,

"The four great beasts are four kingdoms that will rise from the earth." Further clarification on the everlasting kingdom of the Son of Man is in verse eighteen,

> *"But the saints of the Most High will receive*
> *the kingdom and will possess it forever – yes,*
> *forever and ever."*

This is awesome and wonderful news for true believers – those who faithfully follow the Son of Man! God has a wonderful plan for His saints! As He spoke through King David in Psalm 16:13,

> *"As for the saints who are in the land, they are*
> *the glorious ones in whom is all my delight."*

David echoes the Lord's theme in Psalm 101:6,

> *"My eyes will be on the faithful in the land,*
> *that they may dwell with me; he whose walk is*
> *blameless will minister to me."*

You and I can take great comfort today knowing that our God is in control and we will take part in His everlasting Kingdom.

Profiling the Fourth Beast

The rest of Daniel chapter seven concerns the fourth beast in his dream. He asks for and receives an explanation of the "most terrifying" creature of the four. His concerns were the true meaning of this kingdom, the ten horns, the horn that was "more imposing than the others and had eyes and a mouth that spoke boastfully" (Daniel 7:19-20).

Starting in verse twenty-one, we read:

> *"As I watched, this horn was waging war against the saints and defeating them, until the Ancient of Days came and pronounced judgment in favor of the saints of the Most High, and the time came when they possessed the kingdom" (Daniel 7:21-22).*

The explanation begins in verse twenty-three:

> *"The fourth beast is a fourth kingdom that will appear on earth. It will be different from all the other kingdoms and will devour the whole earth, trampling it down and crushing it."*

God goes to great lengths to ensure His people know His truth, even telling us the same thing over and over to be sure we get it! We have already discussed the similarities of Daniel's dream in chapter seven with Nebuchadnezzar's dream in chapter two.

Consider verse twenty-four:

> "The ten horns are ten kings who will come from this kingdom. After them another king will arise, different from the earlier ones; he will subdue three kings."

Revelation 17:12,

> "The ten horns you saw are ten kings who have not yet received a kingdom, but who for one hour will receive authority as kings along with the beast."

Therefore, we see the ten kings coming out of the revised or *revived* Roman Empire. The "antichrist" is different from them and will subdue or overthrow three of its leaders.

Further in Daniel 7:25,

> "He will speak against the Most High and oppress his saints and try to change the set times and the laws. The saints will be handed over to him for a time, times and half a time."

This is a clear picture of what the "beast" of the "Great Tribulation" is about – blaspheming God with lies and false teachings, oppressing and making war against the saints, and changing the Jewish set times and temple laws to demand worship from everyone on planet earth. We know this is the "antichrist" of the book of Revelation – the "beast" of the end of the age – because the next verse in Daniel 7:26 sets the timing as just before the Judgment Day of Almighty God.

Verses twenty-six and twenty-seven say,

> *"But the court will sit, and his power will be taken away and completely destroyed forever."*

We have already discussed from Revelation 19:20 the final judgment of this satanic world leader.

> *"Then the sovereignty, power and greatness of the kingdoms under the whole heaven will be handed over to the saints, the people of the Most High. His kingdom will be an everlasting kingdom, and all rulers will worship and obey him."*

Paul writes in 1 Corinthians 6:2a,

"Do you not know that the saints will judge the world?"

John confirms in Revelation 22:5c,

"And they will reign forever and ever."

Again, our God has a wonderful plan for those who faithfully follow Him. We cannot begin to fathom any of the awesome blessings He has in store for us. As Paul quotes Isaiah in 1 Corinthians 2:9,

"However, as it is written: No eye has seen, no ear has heard, no mind has conceived what God has prepared for those who love him."

A Ram and a Goat

In chapter eight of Daniel, we witness the prophet's next vision. Although this message from the Lord does not directly deal with the "beast" of Revelation thirteen, it does seem to give us a preview. I have already mentioned the dual nature of studying prophecy – the importance of navigating the short-term view and the long-term view. Just as John says in 1 John 2:18,

"Dear children, this is the last hour; and as you have heard that the antichrist is coming, even now many antichrists have come."

We know and understand that down through the ages there have been many to oppose the true Lord God. Many have pridefully rebelled against Him, but ALL have fallen!

Yet, we see in this vision one who behaves and takes action in God's temple much like the last standing "antichrist" of our "end-time" study. A special note of importance is that the Book of Daniel is written in two different languages. Chapter one is in Hebrew, then starting in 2:4 through chapter 7:28, the writing is in Aramaic as the subject matter pertains to the Gentile nations. Chapters eight through twelve return to Hebrew, as this information is vital to the people of Israel and all true believers.

Now let's look closer at Daniel's vision in chapter eight. This one deals with a ram and a goat as its central kingdoms. These kingdoms are identified in verses twenty through twenty-two,

> "The two-horned ram that you saw represents
> the kings of Media and Persia. The shaggy
> goat is the king of Greece, and the large horn
> between his eyes is the first king. The four
> horns that replaced the one that was broken
> off represents four kingdoms that will emerge
> from his nation but will not have the same
> power (Daniel 8:20-22).

Historically, we can see and understand that this revelation concerns the Medo-Persian Empire (two-horned ram) but more importantly, the empire of Alexander the Great or Greece (shaggy goat). He is the first horn; the four horns are the four generals who divided Alexander's empire upon his death. These four kingdoms represent the four horns that "will not have the same power" as he enjoyed.

From this divided rule, the evil king arises. Daniel 8:33-35,

> *"In the latter part of their reign, when rebels have become completely wicked, a stern-faced king, a master of intrigue, will arise. He will become very strong, but not by his own power. He will cause astounding devastation and will succeed in whatever he does. He will destroy the mighty men and the holy people. He will cause deceit to prosper and he will consider himself superior. When they feel secure, he will destroy many and take his stand against the Prince of princes. Yet, he will be destroyed, but not by human power."*

First, we know this passage is not describing the "end-time" antichrist. How? Because this "master of intrigue came from the remains of the "four horns" of Greece. The beast of Revelation thirteen rises out of the "ten toes" of the revived Roman Empire.

Second, this passage almost perfectly describes the ruthless Antiochus IV Epiphanes. He came to power through deceit. He set out in his latter reign to destroy the Jewish people and their faith and demanded to be worshipped as he set himself up as God (Daniel 8:11). He desecrated the sanctuary of the temple in Jerusalem in 168 BC by dedicating the altar to the pagan god Zeus and sacrificing unclean animals. The Lord Almighty raised up Judas Maccabeus and his army to recapture Jerusalem and rededicate the temple in December 165. Antiochus died mysteriously in 164 B.C.

This "completely wicked stern-faced king" is an accurate preview of the coming antichrist of Revelation thirteen. Two main clues – he demands to be worshipped and he desecrates the temple of Jerusalem. This evil ruler (the "master of intrigue") was destroyed, dying from an unknown accident or illness. The "end time" beast will be "thrown alive into the lake of burning sulfur" (Revelation 19:20).

Daniel is instructed in verse twenty-six to "seal up the vision, for it concerns the distant future". As a quick reminder, Daniel lived during the first two great kingdoms – Babylon and Medo-Persia. The kingdom of Greece is to be considered near future. The first Roman Empire is also in the near future. The king who arises from the "ten toes" of the Roman Empire is to be considered "distant future".

A Face like Lightning

Another vision is described in Daniel, chapter ten. Previously, I have covered the teaching of the "Seventy Sevens" found in Daniel

9:20-27, so I won't repeat that here. But I will refer to this teaching of Daniel's "Seventieth Week" in a later chapter to recap.

Daniel's vision of "a man" occurred in the third year of the reign of Cyrus, King of Persia (10:1). The prophet writes,

> *"Its message was true and it concerned a great war" (10:1).*

The message revealed to Daniel covers the rest of his writing through the end of chapter twelve. This vision speaks of a great war with many smaller wars leading up to the final great conflict.

Who is responsible for the revelation Daniel receives in this vision? The answer begins to unfold in verses four through six,

> *"On the twenty-fourth day of the first month, as I was standing on the bank of the great river, the Tigris, I looked up and there before me was a man dressed in linen, with a belt of the finest gold around his waist. His body was like chrysolite, his face like lightning, his eyes like flaming torches, his arms and legs like the gleam of burnished bronze, and his voice like the sound of a multitude."*

Our first clue is the "body of chrysolite." The exact description of this precious stone is unknown – yet it is a part of the high priest of Israel's breastplate (Exodus 28:20). This breastplate was for making decisions in seeking and determining the will of God. This "man dressed in linen with a body of chrysolite" has come to Daniel to reveal the "will of God."

A second clue to his identity is found in Revelation 1:12-16, John writes,

> "I turned around to see the voice that was speaking to me. And when I turned I saw seven golden lampstands, and among the lampstands was someone "like a son of Man, dressed in a robe reaching down to his feet and with a golden sash around his chest. His head and hair were white like wool, as white as snow, and his eyes were like blazing fire. His feet were like bronze glowing in a furnace, and his voice was like the sound of rushing waters. In his right hand he held seven stars, and out of his mouth came a sharp double-edged sword. His face was like the sun shining in all its brilliance".

The robe indicates the high priest; the golden sash points to Jesus Christ as the "Great High Priest." John uses the title "like a son of man", the same one used by Christ in his earthly ministry. The "white head and hair" represent wisdom and dignity. His "blazing eyes", "glowing bronze feet", and "voice of rushing waters" point to the Sovereign who is in charge of all creation. This one is in charge of the "seven stars" held in his right hand, which represent the "angels of the seven churches" (Revelation 1:20). The sharp two-edged sword is the Word of God revealed through Jesus Christ that is symbolized here in divine judgment (Hebrews 4:12).

God has come to Daniel in a very similar way as he appeared to Saul on the road to Damascus (Acts 9:7). The Lord revealed himself to Saul, He revealed himself to Daniel and he desires to reveal himself to you and me today. In chapter ten, Daniel is overwhelmed by this heavenly presence. He is encouraged to "not be afraid" as an explanation has come as to the future of Daniel's people (verse fourteen). Also, the vision will reveal what is written in the "Book of Truth" (verse twenty-one).

This leads us into chapter eleven. The first thirty verses cover the smaller wars of the Ptolemys and Seleucids, who sprang up out of the remains of Alexander the Great's Empire. Most of this information points to a precursor of the "end-time" antichrist. This individual we have already discussed is Antiochus IV Epiphanes, who gave the world a preview of the "abomination that causes desolation" in Daniel 9:27, by dedicating the temple in Jerusalem to the pagan god Zeus.

In Daniel 11:34, we see the close of the information about the smaller wars that lead to this "abomination." We know from history that the temple in Jerusalem was rededicated to the Lord by those led by Judas Maccabeus and his father Mattathias. Therefore, up to this point, this vision has not specifically concerned the antichrist of Revelation thirteen.

Yet, verse thirty-five produces a transition,

> *"Some of the wise will stumble, so that they may be refined, purified and made spotless until the time of the end, for it will still come at the appointed time".*

Thus begins the information concerning the distant future. Daniel 11:36-37 says,

> *"The king will do as he pleases. He will exalt and magnify himself above every god and will say unheard of things against the God of gods. He will be successful until the time of wrath is completed, for what has been determined must take place. He will show no regard for the gods of his fathers or for the one desired by women, nor will he regard any god, but will exalt himself above them all."*

Paul affirms verse thirty-six in 2 Thessalonians 2:4, "He will oppose and will exalt himself over everything that is called God or is worshipped, so that he sets himself up in God's temple, proclaiming himself to be God."

This evil one from Satan (Isaiah 14:12-15) has already been mentioned in Daniel 7:25. "Antichrist" will be successful until the "time of wrath is complete" (Revelation 13:5-8). He will set himself as being above the true and living God.

> *This "beast" will "honor a god of fortresses, a god unknown to his fathers. He will attack the mightiest fortresses with the help of a foreign god. He will honor those who acknowledge him by making them rulers over many people and distributing land at a price" (Daniel 11:38-39).*

This is the "politician of peace," as he is the one who opens the seven year tribulation with "the covenant with many" (Daniel 9:27). He will "change his mind" and "invade many countries and sweep through them like a flood" (11:40).

Antichrist will invade the "Beautiful Land" (Israel). He will extend his power over many countries and gain control of the treasures of gold, silver and all the riches of Egypt. With alarming reports, he sets out in a great rage to destroy and annihilate many (Daniel 11:41-44).

However, he comes to his end in verse forty-five, "He will pitch his royal tents between the seas and the beautiful holy mountain. Yet he will come to his end, and no one will help him. This scene is described fully in Revelation 16:12-16 as the battle of Armageddon. John writes,

"The sixth angel poured out his bowl on the great river Euphrates, and its water was dried up to prepare the way for the kings from the East. Then I saw three evil spirits that looked like frogs; they came out of the mouth of the dragon, out of the mouth of the beast and out of the mouth of the false prophet. They are spirits of demons performing miraculous signs, and they go out to the kings of the whole world, to gather them for the battle on the great day of God Almighty. Behold, I come like a thief! Blessed is he who stays awake and keeps his clothes with him, so that he may not go naked and be shamefully exposed. Then they gathered the kings together to the place that in Hebrew is called Armageddon"

A further description in Revelation 19:19-21 says,

"Then I saw the beast and the kings of the earth and their armies gathered together to make war against the rider on the horse and his army. But the beast was captured, and

216

with him the false prophet who had performed the miraculous signs on his behalf ...The two of them were thrown alive into the fiery lake of burning sulfur. The rest of them were killed with the sword that came out of the mouth of the rider on the horse, and all the birds gorged themselves on their flesh."

On this great terrible day of God Almighty, the followers of antichrist – all of those who are alive and rejected Jesus Christ – and have chosen to follow Satan will meet their doom. With the beast and the false prophet tossed alive in the lake of fire – these are

"thrown into the winepress of God's wrath. They were trampled in the winepress outside the city, and blood flowed out of the press, rising as high as the horse's bridles for a distance of 1,600 stadia" (180 miles). (Revelation 14:19b-20)

How do we know that this figure in Daniel eleven is the real end-time antichrist? Because God continues to confirm this truth in Daniel 12:1,

"At that time Michael, the great prince who protects your people, will arise. There will be a time of distress such as has not happened from

the beginning of nations until then. But at that
time your people – everyone whose name is
found written in the book – will be delivered."

This verse is pointing to the delivering or gathering of the saints (Matthew 24:31). We have already discussed Jesus' central teaching of end time events in Matthew 24. God's Word aligns perfectly with God's Word!

Daniel writes, "Michael will arise," Jesus said that "He will send his angels with a loud trumpet call and they will gather his elect from the four winds, from one end of the heavens to the other." Who will be gathered or delivered? "Everyone whose name is written in the book!" (Daniel 7:10, 12:1, Exodus 32:33, Psalm 69:28, John 20:30, Philippians 4:3, Revelation 3:5, 20:12, 20:15, 21:27)

Daniel 12:2 elaborates,

"Multitudes who sleep in the dust of the earth
will awake; some to everlasting life, others to
shame and everlasting contempt."

This truth is the first clear reference to the resurrection of the dead. This is exactly what Paul teaches in 1 Corinthians 15 – the resurrection of Christ, the resurrection of the dead and the resurrection of the believer. The term "everlasting life" is not found anywhere else in the Old Testament.

Jesus Himself confirms this truth in John 5:24-29.

"I tell you the truth, whoever hears my word and believes him who sent me has eternal life and will not be condemned; he has crossed over from death to life. I tell you the truth, a time is coming and has now come when the dead will hear the voice of the Son of God and those who hear will live. For as the Father has life in himself, so he has granted the Son to have life in Himself. And he has given him authority to judge because he is the Son of Man. Do not be amazed at this, for a time is coming when all who are in their graves will hear his voice and come out – those who have done good will rise to live, and those who have done evil will rise to be condemned."

God's Word continues to confirm and affirm God's Word. You and I must decide - believe the Bible or reject His Truth.

In Daniel 12:3, the one speaking to the prophet gives great encouragement,

"Those who are wise will shine like the brightness of the heavens, and those who lead many to righteousness, like the stars for ever and ever."

One of the many promises of our Lord, this beautiful promise is for those who choose to be faithful and to those who will share their faith in Christ with their fellow man.

The prophet is instructed in verse four to "seal the words of the scroll until the time of the end." Could this scroll be the same scroll of Revelation five? We do know this much – the scroll of Daniel is to be sealed until the time of the end and the scroll of Revelation five is to be opened only by the Lamb – who happens to be the very one who is giving Daniel this vision in Chapters ten through twelve.

Daniel 12: 5-7 continues,

> *"Then I, Daniel, looked, and there before me stood two others, one on this bank of the river and one on the opposite bank. One of them said to the man clothed in linen, who was above the waters of the river, 'How long will it be before these astonishing things are fulfilled?' The man clothed in linen, who was above the waters of the river, lifted his right hand and his left hand toward heaven and I heard him swear by him who lives forever, saying, "It will be for a time, times and half a time"*

In these verses we see a godly oath being taken, which required the minimum of two witnesses. Remember, this is the same vision that started in chapter ten. Also, we are specifically dealing with the evil "end time" king in this section of the vision that began in chapter 11:36. The question "How long?" pertains precisely to the information given about the end-time "beast" or antichrist.

This question is answered by the man clothed in linen – "time, times and half a time." We have already discussed this time frame as being three and half years (Daniel 7:25, 9:27; Revelation 11:2, 13:5). Again, this is specifically speaking of "antichrist" having authority to rule and make war against the saints (God's people) for forty-two months.

In verse eight, Daniel does not understand. However, the man clothed in linen instructs the prophet to, "Go your way, Daniel, because the words are closed up and sealed until the time of the end" (12:9). The one speaking continues to share about the happenings of this time of unparalleled distress (verse two),

> *"Many will be purified, made spotless and refined, but the wicked will continue to be wicked. None of the wicked will understand, but those who are wise will understand", just as in the days of Noah **(Matthew 24:36).***

The wise will understand what? The answer is in verses eleven and twelve,

"From the time that the daily sacrifice is abolished and the abomination that causes desolation is set up, there will be 1290 days" (ref Revelation 11:2). *Blessed is the one who waits for and reaches the end of 1,335 days* (ref Revelation 7:9, 14:17; Matthew 24:29-31).

The answer is as clear as the sky on a sunny day; the true believers are to understand that the "antichrist" is going to have a short time to rule – just forty-two months. As John says in Revelation 13:10b, this calls for patient endurance and faithfulness on the part of the saints." No need to worry or be upset for "Our God Reigns" – "the fifth great kingdom that will never be destroyed", crushes the kingdom of the "antichrist" and brings all kingdoms of the earth to an end (Daniel 2:44-45).

The one dressed in linen concludes this revelation to Daniel by saying,

"As for you, go your way till the end. You will rest, and then at the end of the days you will rise to receive your allotted inheritance (Daniel 12:13)."

What a great word of encouragement and comfort – not only to Daniel but to all who faithfully follow God the Father through

Jesus Christ! We will all face trials, tribulations, temptations, and tests. Yet, as we remain faithful, we – just like Daniel – will "rise to receive our allotted inheritance."

CHAPTER 9

THE PROPHETS AND "THE GREAT TERRIBLE DAY

OF THE LORD"

I now want to focus our attention on the teachings/writings of the Old Testament prophets. In this chapter, we will see clearly the biblical truths concerning God's Judgment Day of planet earth. As we have discussed this "day" (or short time frame) has been called or described by such terms as "time of great distress" (Daniel 12:2, Matthew 24: 21-22); the "great day of the Lord" (Zephaniah 1:14); the "dreadful day of the Lord" (Joel 2:31); the "great day of wrath" (Revelation 6:17); "terrible times" (2 Timothy 3:1); and others too numerous to mention. Therefore, this chapter will certainly not be an exhaustive study, but one that will be profitable and helpful in gaining greater understanding of the second coming of Jesus Christ. We will cover the subject from A to Z, that is, from Amos to Zephaniah. There is certainly not enough time or space to cover every verse pertaining to the "day of the Lord," but we will do our best to hear what the Old Testament prophets had to say about Jesus' second coming.

Let's begin in the book of Amos. This prophet lived during the time of the divided kingdom – Israel in the north and Judah in the south. God sent Amos to announce the coming judgment upon their

225

sins of idolatry, immorality, corruption and oppression of the poor. His prophecy concerned Israel and the nations. A clear picture of judgment against wickedness is found in Amos 5:18-20,

> *"Woe to you who long for the day of the Lord!*
> *Why do you long for the day of the Lord? That*
> *day will be darkness not light. It will be as*
> *though a man fled from a lion only to meet a*
> *bear, as though he entered his house and*
> *rested his hand on the wall only to have a*
> *snake bite him. Will not the day of the Lord be*
> *darkness, not light – pitch-dark, without a ray*
> *of brightness?"*

This word of the Lord through Amos was spoken almost eight hundred years before Christ's first coming!

Yet it aligns perfectly with the description Jesus gave of his return in Matthew 24:29,

> *"Immediately after the distress of those days*
> *the sun will be darkened, and the moon will*
> *not give its light; the stars will fall from the*
> *sky, and the heavenly bodies will be shaken."*

The truth from God's Word is simple – reject God's salvation, practice wickedness, do your own thing, and this day will come upon you like a thief in the night (1 Thessalonians 5:2). Amos further declares in 8:9,

> "In that day, declares the Sovereign Lord, I will make the sun go down at noon and darken the earth in broad daylight."

For those who remain faithful – do not despair – because this "day of the Lord" will be our day of redemption. Amos 9:11-12 says:

> "In that day I will restore David's fallen tent. I will repair its broken places, restore its ruins, and build it as it used to be, so that they may possess the remnant of Edom and all the nations that hear my name, declares the Lord, who will do these things."

We see affirmation from Daniel about this time of great distress at the hand of the antichrist until God's judgment day begins. In Daniel 7:21-22 we read,

> "As I watched, this horn was waging war against the saints and defeating them, until the Ancient of Days came and pronounced judgment in favor of the saints of the Most High, and the time came when they possessed the kingdom."

What a glorious time – in spite of all of the devil's tribulation. God's people will receive the rewards of their faithfulness and possess the kingdom of our only Lord and Savior – Jesus Christ!

David: The Psalmist

Looking into the book of Psalms we see that on several occasions the Psalmist pointed to the day of God's judgment. In Psalm 1:5, the author writes,

> *"Therefore the wicked will not stand in the judgment, nor sinners in the assembly of the righteous."*

The contrast here is with verse two,

> *"But his delight is in the law of the Lord, and on his law he meditates day and night." When God's day of wrath comes, the faithful – those who delight in the Lord's word – will have nothing to fear. However, the wicked will fall and they will have no place in God's kingdom.*

In Psalm 9, David speaks of that day:

> *"The Lord reigns forever; he has established his throne for judgment. He will judge the world in righteousness; he will govern the*

peoples with justice. The Lord is a refuge for the oppressed, a stronghold in times of trouble. Those who know your name will trust in you, for you, Lord, have never forsaken those who seek you" (9:7-10).

Believers will have nothing to fear on the day of God's wrath. Those who have received the righteousness of Christ will take refuge in the rapture. As David says in verse ten, "you Lord, have never forsaken those who seek you." Those who trust in the Lord Almighty and the Lamb will never be put to shame (Romans 9:33, Isaiah 28:16). Jesus confirms this day in Matthew 13:49-50,

"This is how it will be at the end of the age. The angels will come and separate the wicked from the righteous and throw them into the fiery furnace, where there will be weeping and gnashing of teeth."

David speaks the truth when he says the Lord will judge the world in righteousness. God is a perfect being – everything He does is perfect. Jesus speaks again of the Judgment Day in Matthew 25:31-32,

"When the Son of Man comes in his glory, and the angels with him, he will sit on his throne in heavenly glory. All the nations will be

gathered before him, and he will separate the people one from another as a shepherd separates the sheep from the goats."

David closes out Psalm 9 with this prayer in verses nineteen and twenty,

"Arise, O Lord, let not man triumph; let the nations be judged in your presence. Strike them with terror, O Lord; let the nations know they are but men."

In Psalm 98, the writer calls the people of God to rejoice at the coming of the righteous reign of our Lord. In verses one and two, we discover,

"Sing to the Lord a new song, for he has done marvelous things; his right hand and his holy arm have worked salvation for him. The Lord has made his salvation known and revealed his righteousness to the nations."

The marvelous things in verse one are related directly to the salvation that Messiah will bring. Luke quotes Isaiah 40:3-5, in reference to John the Baptist preparing the way of the Lord – the coming of Jesus Christ (Luke 3:4-6). Isaiah 52:10 affirms Psalm 98:2,

"The Lord will lay bare his holy arm in the sight of all nations, and all the ends of the earth will see the salvation of our God."

When Jesus was presented for circumcision as a baby, the righteous and devout

"Simeon took him in his arms and praised God, saying: 'Sovereign Lord, as you have promised, you now dismiss your servant in peace. For my eyes have seen your salvation, which you have prepared in the sight of all people, a light for revelation to the Gentiles and for glory to your people Israel" (Luke 2:28-32).

To this man Simeon, the truth had been revealed (by the Holy Spirit) that he would not die before he had seen the Lord's Christ (Luke 2:26). Thus, he was ready in the temple courts for the arrival of his Messiah. This is an awesome reminder for you and me today – as Jesus said in Matthew 24:44,

"So you also must be ready, because the Son of Man will come at an hour when you do not expect him."

With the salvation of our Lord revealed, no wonder the Psalmist calls out to God's people to rejoice. The last two verses of

Psalm 98 bless us with a beautiful picture of celebration at the coming of our Messiah. Verses nine and ten proclaim,

> *"Let the rivers clap their hands, let the mountains sing together for joy; let them sing before the Lord, for he comes to judge the earth. He will judge the world in righteousness and the peoples with equity."*

Selah! Praise His Holy Name.

Ezekiel's Role in End Time Prophecy

The prophet Ezekiel's focus was primarily concerned with Israel. However, God did pronounce judgment on the nations through Ezekiel in chapters twenty-five through thirty-two. As early as chapter seven the prophet receives a divine glimpse of the "day of the Lord",

> *"Doom has come upon you – you who dwell in the land. The time has come, the day is near; there is panic, not joy, upon the mountains". I am about to pour out my wrath on you and spend my anger against you; I will judge you according to your conduct and repay your for all your detestable practices"* (Ezekiel 7:7-8).

This brief glimpse of God's future wrath matches up exactly with Jesus' warnings in Matthew 24: 9-25 and John's vision of the judgment of seals in Revelation 6: 1-17.

Also in chapter thirty verses two and three, we read,

> *"Son of man, prophesy and say: This is what the Sovereign Lord says: Wail and say, Alas for that day! For the day is near, a day of clouds, a time of doom for the nations."*

The Lord spoke to Ezekiel concerning the short-term prophecy against Egypt as a preview of the final "day of the Lord". This prophecy aligns with Joel 2:2 and Zephaniah 1:15 and certainly can be seen in John's revelation of the wrath of God being poured out on all the nations who rejected the Lamb.

The last passage we will examine in Ezekiel is 32:7-8. The Lord is speaking,

> *"When I snuff you out, I will cover the heavens and darken their stars; I will cover the sun with a cloud, and the moon will not give its light. All the shining lights in the heavens I will darken over you; I will bring darkness over your land, declares the Sovereign Lord."*

This passage matches up with Isaiah 13:10, 34:4; Joel 2:2, 31, 3:15; Matthew 24:29 and Revelation 6:12, 13 and 8:12. These verses are usually referred to as the signs that begin the "terrible day of "God's wrath/judgment". Every follower of Jesus Christ should know these signs because they alert us to His coming! Jesus said in Matthew 24:29,

> *"Immediately after the distress of those days –*
> *the sun will be darkened, and the moon will*
> *not give its light; the stars will fall from the*
> *sky, and the heavenly bodies will be shaken."*

When all of the things come together as Jesus taught in Matthew 24 – antichrist is revealed (the abomination that causes desolation), Satan's wrath is over, the day of the Gentile is complete – these signs of darkness will signal that the "day of the Lord" has arrived. The very first appointment on God's "judgment day" is the "gathering of his elect from the four winds" (Matthew 24:31). We'll talk about this in a later chapter.

The Importance of Hosea

Looking in the book of Hosea we see a most important verse that answers or corrects an error in our thinking as students of end-time prophecy. Hosea 3:5 reads, *"Afterward the Israelites will return and seek the Lord their God and David their king. They will come trembling to the Lord and to his blessings in the last days."*

This prophecy is a Messianic prediction – "the Israelites will return seeking the Lord and their Davidic king... in the last days."

There are some who teach that God finished dealing with Israel at the close of Jesus' first coming. However, Hosea 3:5 agrees with Paul's claim that all true Israel will be saved (Romans 11:26). Who is "true" Israel? All those who put their trust and faith in the greatest of all the Jews – Jesus Christ. Paul says in Romans 3:21-23,

> *"But now righteousness from God, apart from the law, has been made known, to which the Law and the Prophets testify. This righteousness from God comes through faith in Jesus Christ to all who believe. There is no difference, for all have sinned and fall short of the glory of God."*

Jesus said in Matthew 24:14a,

> *"And this Gospel of the kingdom will be preached in the whole world as a testimony to all nations."*

God here is actively sending his message to all nations. In Revelation 7:3-4,

> *"Do not harm the land or the sea or the trees until we put a seal on the foreheads of the servants of our God. Then I heard the number*

of those who were sealed: 144,000 from all the
tribes of Israel."

Regardless of what role these servants have – the Lord God of Israel is still seeking those who will be saved – including those from the house of Israel.

What the Book of Isaiah Reveals

This prophet has much to say concerning the great and terrible "day of the Lord". Yet we will focus our attention on the most applicable to our study. In the vast prophecies of the sixty-six chapters, the Lord revealed the following to Isaiah, early in chapter two – verses 11, 17, 18, 19 and 20. Isaiah 2:11,

> *"The eyes of the arrogant man will be*
> *humbled and the pride of men brought low;*
> *the Lord alone will be exalted in that day."*

The theme continues in verses seventeen and eighteen,

> *"The arrogance of man will be brought low*
> *and the pride of men humbled; the Lord alone*
> *will be exalted in that day, and the idols will*
> *totally disappear. Verse nineteen continues,*
> *"Men will flee to caves in the rocks, and to*
> *holes in the ground from dread of the Lord*

and the splendor of his majesty, when he rises
to shake the earth."

This prophecy aligns perfectly with Revelation 6:15-17,

"Then the kings of the earth, the princes, the
generals, the rich, the mighty, and every slave
and every free man hid in caves and among
the rocks of the mountains. They called to the
mountains and the rocks - fall on us and hide
us from the face of him who sits on the throne
and from the wrath of the Lamb! For the great
day of their wrath has come and who can
stand?"

Isaiah 2:20-21 says:

"In that day, men will throw away to the
rodents and rats their idols of silver and idols
of gold, which they made to worship. They will
flee to caverns in the rocks and to the
overhanging crags from dread of the Lord and
the splendor of his majesty, when he rises to
shake the earth".

The picture from this theme of Isaiah chapter two is so tragic.
These people who rejected Messiah now – run from the one who

loves them most. The tragedy is that their opportunity to repent and receive forgiveness is over – the day of God's judgment has come.

The phrase "splendor of his majesty" relates to Jesus' words in Matthew 24:30,

> *"At that time the sign of the Son of Man will appear in the sky, and all the nations of the earth will mourn. They will see the Son of Man coming on the clouds of the sky, with power and great glory."*

For believers, this day will be indescribably wonderful. But for unbelievers this day will be terror beyond description.

Another of God's warnings closes Isaiah two. In verse twenty-two we read,

> *"Stop trusting in man, who has but a breath in his nostrils. Of what account is he?"*

This verse relates to the rejection of the Messiah in Isaiah 53:3. God provides the perfect leader – the only one worthy – only for rebellious, sinful mankind to reject him. Sadly, this rejection is to their eternal doom.

In Isaiah thirteen we see another description of this coming judgment. In verses nine and ten,

"See, the day of the Lord is coming – a cruel day, with wrath and fierce anger – to make the land desolate and destroy the sinners within it. The stars of heaven and their constellations will not show their light. The rising sun will be darkened and the moon will not give its light."

A couple of truths jump out at me. One, God's judgment day will not touch the believers – only sinners – those who have rejected God's Son. A second thought is the recurring theme of the sign of that day – total darkness. As I said earlier in this chapter – all believers should know that the sign that begins God's judgment day is when the sun, moon and stars give no light. When this great cosmic phenomenon occurs – Jesus Christ will appear.

Chapters 24-27 of Isaiah deal with God's blessings and judgment in the last days. This prophecy of end-time events describes the final victory over the Lord's evil enemies. I want to encourage you to begin to study Isaiah, Daniel and the prophets in depth because when we gain greater understanding of the Old Testament teachings, then we will have greater understanding of the New Testament teachings of Christ and the Apostles. Time and space do not permit us to examine these four chapters. However, I would like to point out a few key verses.

God reassures through Isaiah that His judgment will be directed at those who have rejected His Word. In Isaiah 24:3,

> *"The earth will be completely laid waste and totally plundered. The Lord has spoken this word."*

Why? The answer is in verse five,

> *"The earth is defiled by its people; they have disobeyed the laws, violated the statutes and broken the everlasting covenant."*

The rest of chapter twenty-four describes what it will be like on planet earth at this time. Interestingly, a recurring theme appears again in the last verse. Isaiah 24:3,

> *"The moon will be abashed, the sun ashamed; for the Lord Almighty will reign on Mount Zion and in Jerusalem and before its elders, gloriously."*

This verse begins with the sun and moon darkened during God's final judgment as found in the Matthew twenty-four teaching of Jesus. Then this prophecy points directly to the millennial reign of Christ as found in Revelation 20:1-6.

Isaiah twenty-five and twenty-six burst into songs of praise to the Lord for His awesome and wonderful deliverance. As we move into chapter twenty-seven, God opens in verse one with the phrase, "In that day." He is again reassuring His people of their deliverance from all the nations who have oppressed them. Isaiah 27:12-13 repeats the promise of 24:23 when the Lord rules and reigns from Jerusalem.

> *"In that day the Lord will thresh from the flowing Euphrates to the Wadi of Egypt, and you, O Israelites, will be gathered up one by one. And in that day a great trumpet will sound. Those who were perishing in Assyria and those who were exiled in Egypt will come and worship the Lord on the holy mountain in Jerusalem".*

I want us to pause for a moment to consider the enormity of our God. Isaiah wrote roughly seven hundred years before Christ spoke the words of Matthew twenty-four! And yet, Isaiah 27:12-13 is a perfect description of Christ's teaching of the "gathering of the elect from the four winds" (Matthew 24:31). What an awesome God.

Jeremiah Speaks to the Last Days

Jeremiah, often called the "weeping prophet," was a fearless preacher of righteousness in his day. His ministry began in 626 BC and lasted about forty years. While most of his attention was directed at Israel, particularly Judah, he does speak to the "last days" of God's final judgment against all the evil, rebellious nations of earth.

The Lord speaks words of tenderness and encouragement through this fiery prophet. Consider Jeremiah 3:15-18:

> *"Then I will give you shepherds after my own heart, who will lead you with knowledge and understanding. In those days, when your numbers have increased greatly in the land, declares the Lord, men will no longer say, 'The ark of the covenant of the Lord'. It will never enter their minds or be remembered; it will not be missed, nor will another one be made. At that time they will call Jerusalem the Throne of the Lord, and all nations will gather in Jerusalem to honor the name of the Lord. No longer will they follow the stubbornness of their evil hearts. In those days the house of Judah will join the house of Israel, and together they will come from a northern land to the land I gave your forefathers as an inheritance."*

This passage describes the time of Messiah's reign. There will be shepherds or teacher/leaders who will point the people to Christ with knowledge and understanding of Him. The Ark of the Covenant will be obsolete, as Messiah has come to make His Royal Presence known to all the nations. These nations – yes all the nations of earth – will call Jerusalem the Throne of the Lord and will gather to honor his Holy Name. What name? Paul answers in Philippians 2:9-11,

> *"Therefore God exalted him to the highest place and gave him the name that is above every name, that at the name of Jesus every knee should bow, in heaven and on earth and under the earth, and every tongue confess that Jesus Christ is Lord, to the glory of God the Father."*

In this time of Messiah – the people will choose Christ and stop following their evil, stubborn ways. Both houses of Israel will dwell in unity in the land that God gave them.

What a beautiful promise from our Lord. In spite of the ever-increasing evil culminating with "antichrist's" time of authority – God's people – those who truly believe in Jesus Christ – have a wonderful and awesome future. In Jeremiah 29:11 the Lord speaks this promise,

"For I know the plans I have for you, declares the Lord, plans to prosper you and not to harm you, plans to give you a hope and a future."

This theme of tribulation/restoration is also seen in Jeremiah 30:7-11a.

"How awful that day will be! None will be like it. It will be a time of trouble for Jacob, but he will be saved out of it. In that day, declares the Lord Almighty, I will break the yoke off their necks and will tear off their bonds; no longer will foreigners enslave them. Instead, they will serve the Lord their God and David their king, whom I will raise up for them. So do not fear, O Jacob my servant; do not be dismayed, O Israel, declares the Lord. I will surely save you out of a distant place, your descendants from the land of their exile. Jacob will again have peace and security, and no one will make him afraid. I am with you and will save you, declares the Lord."

This passage begins with the "awful day" that "none will be like it." This is in direct relationship to Jesus' teachings in Matthew 24:21,

> *"For then there will be great distress, unequaled from the beginning of the world until now – and never to be equaled again."*

This great tribulation period brought on by "antichrist" is going to be a time of trouble for Israel and all believers. But the Lord saves the elect out of it before His holy judgment falls on the rebellious inhabitants of earth. Verse eight is a transition verse as the Lord breaks the bondage of Jacob's foreign slavery (transition from tribulation to Messiah's reign). Instead, (verse nine) Jacob will serve the Lord and David their king. Of course, the phrase "David their king" refers directly to Messiah. The rest of the passage is used by God to reassure Jacob/Israel. He uses phrases like: "do not fear"; "do not be dismayed"; "I will surely save you"; "Jacob will again have peace and security"; "no one will make him afraid"; "I am with you and will save you." These phrases give us a clue as to when these things will transpire. *This passage speaks clearly to the thousand-year reign of Messiah.* The best clue is found in the phrase "Jacob will again have peace and security." Most bible students know that true, lasting peace and security for Israel and all the nations will come only when Jesus Christ, the Prince of Peace, comes and establishes His rule.

A Different Perspective from the Prophet Joel

This mostly obscure prophet brings us a different perspective of the "great day of the Lord." Joel is not mentioned anywhere in Scripture, except here and Acts 2:16-21, where Peter quotes a prophecy found in chapter 2:28-32. In Joel 1:15 we read,

> *"Alas for that day! For the day of the Lord is near; it will come like destruction from the Almighty."*

The phrase "day of the Lord" is used five times in this short prophecy of three chapters. However, this phrase is used by Isaiah (13:6,9); Amos (5:18,20); Malachi (4:5); Zephaniah (1:7,14); Obadiah (15) and Ezekiel (13:5, 30:3).

Joel sees (in the short term prophetic view) locusts coming to destroy the land because of Israel's disobedience and unwillingness to repent. His long term prophetic view of the day of the Lord aligns with the signs given by Jesus in Matthew 24:39. In Joel 2:10, 11 the locusts are coming and the prophet writes,

> *"Before them the earth shakes, the sky trembles, the sun and moon are darkened and the stars no longer shine ... The day of the Lord is great; it is dreadful. Who can endure it?"*

The prophet is foreshadowing the great day of God's final judgment with the soon arrival of the army of locusts. The thought from verse eleven goes perfectly with the question raised in Revelation 6:17,

> *"For the great day of their wrath has come,*
> *and who can stand?"*

John, of course, is speaking of the One who sits on the throne and the Lamb (Revelation 6:16).

In chapter two we discover the passage that Peter quotes on the Day of Pentecost in Acts 2:16-21. Look at the promises of God in the five verses of Joel 2:28-32a:

> *"And afterward, I will pour out my Spirit on all people. Your sons and daughters will prophesy, your old men will dream dreams, your young men will see visions. Even on my servants, both men and women, I will pout out my Spirit in those days. I will show wonders in the heavens and on the earth, blood and fire and billows of smoke. The sun will be turned to darkness and the moon to blood before the coming of the great and dreadful day of the Lord. And everyone who calls on the name of the Lord will be saved."*

In verse twenty-eight, the word "afterward" means after the days of the locust. The time frame of this prophecy is after God restores the land to the repentant house of Israel in Joel's day. Peter applies this prophecy to the day of Pentecost, a glorious day of God pouring out of His Spirit and taking His message to the world. In a previous chapter we discussed the biblical view of "the last days." We see and understand from the New Testament writers that the "last days" began with Jesus' ascension in Acts chapter one. The true believers received Jesus' promise of the coming of the Holy Spirit as "God poured out His Spirit."

In these "last days" – the time of the church – God has poured out his Spirit. His sons and daughters have preached his Word. Old men have had dreams and young men have seen visions – with the purpose of "preaching this Gospel of the kingdom to the whole world as a testimony to all nations, and then the end will come" (Matthew 24:14).

All these things lead up to the "great day of the Lord", which will open with the "wonders in the heavens, blood, fire and billows of smoke." These wonders are revealed in the sun going dark and the moon turning to blood which are the exact signs Jesus predicted would begin the great day of God's final judgment. Also, we see wonderful news in verse twenty-two,

> *"And everyone who calls on the name of the*
> *Lord will be saved."*

This is why it is so vitally important that we, Christians of today, get the Gospel to all nations – giving all peoples an opportunity to "call on the name of the Lord" – the Lord Jesus Christ.

Joel 3:15-16 echoes this very obvious theme. The pattern through the prophets is simple – sin/rebellion, judgment, restoration of/for those who repent or for those who "call on the name of the Lord." Joel 3:15-16 says,

> *"The sun and moon will be darkened, and the stars no longer shine. The Lord will roar from Zion and thunder from Jerusalem; the earth and sky will tremble. But the Lord will be a refuge for his people, a stronghold for the people of Israel."*

In verse fifteen, our God repeats for the umpteenth time the signs of His Coming. You might be tempted to say, "Enough already with the signs of the sun, moon and stars!" But I want you to see how gracious and merciful our Lord really is – that He repeats these signs over and over – through the prophets – through the apostles – He himself even told us in his Gospels (Matthew 24:29, Luke 21:25, Mark 13:24), so there would be no confusion and no excuse, so that no one would miss out on being ready when Christ comes for his people.

After the final "day of the Lord", comes the final restoration period - the 1,000-year rule and reign of Messiah. Truly, the Lord will be a refuge to his people. We close with Joel 3:17,

> *"Then you will know that I, the Lord your God,*
> *dwell in Zion, my holy hill. Jerusalem will be*
> *holy; never again will foreigners invade her."*

With Jesus Christ seated on "The Throne" in Jerusalem, God's people will surely dwell in peace, security and bounty. John, in Revelation 20:6, writes of this period,

> *"Blessed and holy are those who have part in*
> *the first resurrection. The second death has no*
> *power over them, but they will be priests of*
> *God and of Christ and will reign with him for a*
> *thousand years."*

Malachi's Last Days' Words

This prophet, whose writing closes out the Old Testament, has a couple of points of interest for our study. The coming of Messiah that opens "the day of the Lord" has a two-fold purpose according to Malachi. One, to refine the believer, as found in Malachi 3:2-4,

> *"But who can endure the day of his coming?*
> *Who can stand when he appears? For he will*

be like a refiners fire or a launderer's soap. He
will sit as a refiner and purifier of silver; he
will purify the Levites and refine them like
gold and silver. Then the Lord will have men
who will bring offerings in righteousness, and
the offerings of Judah and Jerusalem will be
acceptable to the Lord, as in days gone by, as
in former years."

Messiah will come and purify the house of Israel through the time of great distress. Christ will cleanse the Levites, the messengers, or servants, of God. Thus, producing offerings of righteousness that will again be acceptable to a holy God as in days gone by.

Secondly, there is a focus on the judgment of the wicked. The prophet writes in Malachi 4:1,

"Surely the day is coming; it will burn like a
furnace. All the arrogant and every evil doer
will be stubble, and that day that is coming
will set them on fire, says the Lord Almighty.
Not a root or branch will be left to them".

Compare this verse of doom for the evildoer to the joy of the believer in 4:2,

"But for you who revere my name, the sun of righteousness will rise with healing in its wings. And you will go out and leap like calves released from the stall."

The rebellious and arrogant that reject Christ become as stubble in a tremendous furnace. However, those who are purified and revere God's Name will run free like calves released from their stalls.

One last point from Malachi 4:5,

"See, I will send you the prophet Elijah before that great and dreadful day of the Lord comes." Most Bible students know that Elijah never tasted death (2 Kings 2:11),

"As they were walking along and talking together, suddenly a chariot of fire and horses of fire appeared and separated the two of them, and Elijah went up to heaven in a whirlwind"). Some might say that John the Baptist was Elijah, but John 1:21 clears up that falsehood, "They asked him, 'Then who are you? Are you Elijah?' He said, 'I am not.'"

The Jews believed that Elijah would return to announce "the day of the Lord", as prophesied in this Malachi 4:5 verse. Also, Elijah appeared with Moses on the mount of transfiguration. Matthew 17:1-2,

> *"After six days Jesus took with him Peter, James and John the brother of James, and led them up a high mountain by themselves. There he was transfigured before them. His face shown like the sun, and his clothes became as white as the light. Just then there appeared before them Moses and Elijah, talking with Jesus."*

Based on these two scriptures, I believe Elijah will be one of the two witnesses of Revelation 11:3:

> *"And I will give power to my two witnesses, and they will prophecy for 1,260 days, clothed in sackcloth."*

Elijah will come before the "great and dreadful day of the Lord" to prepare God's people for the Coming of Jesus Christ.

The Role of Micah and Obadiah in Prophecy

Most of what these two prophets have today deals with the short-term prophetic view of the nation of Israel. However, both give us glimpses into the Messianic era – the 1,000 year reign of Jesus Christ. In Micah 4:6-7,

"In that day, declares the Lord, I will gather
the lame; I will assemble the exiles and those I
have brought to grief. I will make the lame a
remnant, those driven away a strong nation.
The Lord will rule over them in Mount Zion
from that day and forever."

Obadiah 17 agrees, "But on Mount Zion will be deliverance; it will be holy and the house of Jacob will possess its inheritance."

Yet, there is final judgment through both prophets. Micah 5:10a, 11, 15;

"In that day, declares the Lord. I will destroy
the cities of your land and tear down all your
strongholds. I will take vengeance in anger
and wrath upon the nations that have not
obeyed me."

Obadiah 15 concurs,

"The day of the Lord is near for all nations. As
you have done, it will be done to you; your
deeds will return upon your own head."

Zechariah's Eye-Opening Statements

With Zechariah's writing, we receive better understanding of the fulfillment of the promise to Abraham in 2:10 11a:

254

*"Shout and be glad, O daughter of Zion. For I
am coming, and I will be among you, declares
the Lord. Many nations will be joined with the
Lord in that day and will become my people."*

This prophecy of Messiah connects the promise of Abraham
that all nations would be blessed through him (Genesis 12:3) with
the time of Revelation 20:6 when Jesus dwells among his people.

In chapter fourteen we see some interesting things
happening on the "day of the Lord". Verse one says,

*"A day of the Lord is coming." Verse two says,
"I will gather the nations to Jerusalem to fight
against it." And in verse three we read, "Then
the Lord will go out and fight against those
nations." Verse four adds, "On that day his feet
will stand on the Mount of Olives" and "the
Mount of Olives will be split in two." Verse five
says, "Then the Lord my God will come, and all
the holy ones with him." And verse nine reads:
"The Lord will be King over the whole earth.
On that day there will be one Lord and his
name the only name." (Revelation 19:11-21)
These verses line up consistently with the
biblical information we have already*

discussed. God's Word always confirms God's Word.

Even Zephaniah Talks About the Last Days

Last, but certainly not least, we hear from the prophet Zephaniah. In three relatively short chapters, the Lord speaks clearly through this prophet roughly 600 years before Christ's first coming. In chapter one, verses fourteen through sixteen we read,

> *"The great day of the Lord is near – near and coming quickly. Listen! The cry of the day of the Lord will be bitter, the shouting of the warrior there. That day will be a day of wrath, a day of distress and anguish, a day of trouble and ruin, a day of darkness and gloom, a day of clouds and blackness, a day of trumpet and battle cry against the fortified cities and against the corner towers." Zephaniah further warns in verse eighteen, "Neither their silver nor their gold will be able to save them on the day of the Lord's wrath."*

Thankfully, there is good news on this very dark day. To the believer, God says in 3:17,

"The Lord your God is with you, he is mighty to save. He will take delight in you, he will quiet you with his love, he will rejoice over you with singing."

More good news is revealed in 3:19-20:

"At that time I will deal with all who oppressed you; I will rescue the lame and gather those have been scattered. I will give them praise and honor in every land where they were put to shame. At that time I will gather you; at that time I will bring you home. I will give you honor and praise among all the peoples of the earth when I restore your fortunes before your very eyes, says the Lord."
Amen!

From this brief chapter concerning the prophets' view of that "great day" we see clearly that each one is speaking of the return of Jesus Christ. The Old Testament and New Testament are in perfect harmony. For the Old Testament prophet, Jesus was their long awaited Messiah. For the New Testament Apostle – Christ is their risen KING. The great news for believers today is that these two – Messiah and King – are one and the same!

"Hear, O Israel: The Lord our God, the Lord is One" (Deuteronomy 6:4). *Jesus seals this truth in John 10:30, saying to all who have ears to hear: "I and the Father are One."*

CHAPTER 10

THE APOSTLE PAUL AND "THE GREAT TERRIBLE

DAY OF THE LORD"

In the previous chapter, we examined some of the writings of the Old Testament prophets concerning "the day of the Lord." In this chapter, we will examine two important writings from Paul. Hopefully, this chapter will help us gain greater insight and wisdom concerning the timing of "end time" events.

The apostle Paul was one of the leading writers of the New Testament. He is responsible for Romans, first and second Corinthians, Galatians, Ephesians, Philippians, Timothy, Titus and Philemon. Most of Paul's writings were in response to a question or problem in one of the local churches he planted during his missionary journeys.

We see in the book of 1 Thessalonians, Paul addressing a question concerning "the coming of the Lord." Also, in his second letter to the church at Thessalonica Paul answers another "end time" question about the "antichrist." Here, I want to pause to encourage you to open your mind and heart to the Holy Spirit and ask Him to guide and direct your thinking as you encounter Paul's teachings about the "coming of our Lord." This could revolutionize your entire view of the "end of the age."

Now let's investigate I Thessalonians 4:13-18:

> *"Brothers, we do not want you to be ignorant about those who fall asleep, or to grieve like the rest of men, who have no hope. We believe that Jesus died and rose again and so we believe that God will bring with Jesus those who have fallen asleep in him. According to the Lord's own word, we tell you that we who are still alive, who are left till the coming of the Lord, will certainly not precede those who have fallen asleep. For the Lord himself will come down from heaven, with a loud command, with the voice of the archangel and the trumpet call of God, and the dead in Christ shall rise first. After that, we who are still alive and are left will be caught up together with them in the clouds to meet the Lord in the air. And so we will be with the Lord forever. Therefore encourage each other with these words."*

The question, "What happens to those who are physically dead when Jesus returns?" had been raised. It is a very valid concern and I am grateful someone had the insight and courage to ask. "Would the 'dead' miss out on the 'great resurrection day'?" In verse thirteen, Paul begins to clarify the correct biblical position. He writes,

"Brothers, we do not want you to be ignorant about those who fall asleep, or to grieve like the rest of men, who have no hope."

In essence, Paul is saying, "Church, listen up, for this is the correct teaching from the Lord." He emphasizes that he wants the church to know the truth about Jesus' second coming. Paul encourages the reader that we do not need to be concerned about our loved ones who have preceded us in death. We, who believe in Christ, do not grieve like those who are lost spiritually. Because of Jesus' resurrection – we have hope. The individual, who rejects Christ, has no hope in death. The only future for this person is the judgment fire of hell as he or she will be eternally separated from God and all of those who love Him. What greater motivation do we need? When we accept Jesus Christ as our substitute for our sin – we can look forward to spending eternity in his presence! There's more! We will also share this forever experience with all of the believers throughout history! When I preach a funeral service of a believer, I always remind those present that they can see their loved one again. But there is only one doorway – Jesus Christ! He said in John 14:6, *"I am the way and the truth and the life. No one comes to the Father except through me."* Therefore, Paul is comforting and encouraging his readers to take hope in the power of Jesus' resurrection.

Here it is in verse fourteen,

> *"We believe that Jesus died and rose again and so we believe that God will bring with Jesus those who have fallen asleep in him."*

The Lord shows no favoritism, as Peter said in Acts 10:34-35,

> *"...I now realize how true it is that God does not show favoritism but accepts men from every nation who fear him and do what is right".*

Paul states this truth in Romans 2:11,

> *"For God does not show favoritism."*

Based on this teaching found both in the Old Testament (Exodus 23:3, Leviticus 19:15) and the New Testament – God would not favor the living over those who had died in Christ. The prophet Daniel even states in chapter twelve, verse two,

"Multitudes who sleep in the dust of the earth will awake: some to everlasting life, others to shame and everlasting contempt."

Based on the fact that Jesus died and rose again – believers will follow His lead or pattern and do likewise. Paul teaches in Romans 14:9,

"For this very reason, Christ died and returned to life so that He might be the Lord of the dead and the living."

Christ has Lordship over both the dead and the living because of His victory over death through the power of his resurrection. Paul continues in verses fifteen and sixteen,

"According to the Lord's own word, we tell you that we who are still alive, who are left till the coming of the Lord, will certainly not precede those who have fallen asleep. For the Lord Himself will come down from heaven with a loud command, with the voice of the archangel and with the trumpet call of God, and the dead in Christ will rise first."

Our God does not forget. He is perfect. His mercy is greater than any and all human wisdom, intelligence and justice. The Lord

God Creator will not forget His own – be they physically dead or alive. Jesus confirms this 1 Thessalonians 4 passage in John 5:24-25,

> "I tell you the truth, whoever hears my word and believes him who sent me has eternal life and will not be condemned; he has crossed over from death to life. I tell you the truth, a time is coming and has now come when the dead will hear the voice of the Son of God and those who hear will live."

Jesus is teaching a two-fold truth concerning his ministry. First,

> "All who hear and believe in Christ receive eternal life and will not be condemned." Secondly, "a time is coming when the dead will hear the voice of the Son of God and will live."

This is a direct reference to the "rapture" of the saints or the great "resurrection day," because, the "rapture" and the "resurrection day" are one and the same event (Matthew 24:31).

Jesus goes on to say in John 5:28-29,

> "Do not be amazed at this, for a time is coming when all who are in their graves will hear his voice and come out – those who have done

good will rise to live, and those who have done
evil will rise to be condemned."

What is the greatest good one could do? Simply accepting God's great gift of salvation through His Son Jesus Christ! What would be the greatest evil one could do? Offending God by rejecting His great gift of salvation through His Son. John affirms this truth in Revelation 20:5-6,

> *"The rest of the dead did not come to life until the thousand years were ended. Blessed and holy are those who have part in the first resurrection. The second death has no power over them, but they will be priests of God and of Christ and will reign with him for a thousand years."*

Paul is clarifying for the Thessalonians that at the "first resurrection" which Jesus called "resurrection of the righteous" in Luke 14:4 – the dead in Christ shall rise first. The second resurrection is the raising of all the wicked dead at the "great white throne" judgment found in Revelation 20:11-15. Allow me to ask you a personal question. If you were to die today, which resurrection would you take part in?

It is not a difficult decision – the people at the first resurrection are blessed and will serve and rule with Jesus forever

(Revelation 22:5b). However, at the second resurrection – it will be too late to change your mind! Your name must be written in the "Book of Life" before you physically die. The only way to have your name written in this awesome "Book of Life" is to repent of your sin and receive God's greatest gift – salvation through His Son Jesus Christ. If you have never done this – please stop and take a moment right now to invite Jesus into your life. Ask Him to forgive you of all your sins and give you eternal life! This is the Creator's desire – a personal and intimate relationship with His creation – just as he had with Adam and Eve in the garden before sin separated all human beings from Him (Genesis 3:8-9).

Back to the 1 Thessalonians 4 passage. Paul states in verses seventeen and eighteen, "After that, we who are still alive and are left will be caught up together with them in the clouds to meet the Lord in the air. And so we will be with the Lord forever. Therefore encourage each other with these words."

Consider the question in verse seventeen, "After what?" After the dead in Christ have risen first – immediately all the believers in Christ who are still physically alive will be "caught up" together with them in the clouds to meet Jesus in the air. From this point in time throughout all eternity – all believers will be in the presence of God.

This is great and wonderful news! No wonder Paul writes in verse eighteen for believers to "encourage each other with these words." Just as Jesus said in Matthew 24:29, this event, "the resurrection of the righteous" would take place immediately after the distress of "Satan's" wrath. Therefore, the "rapture" (Matthew 24:31) or the "first resurrection" (Revelation 20:6) will be THE EVENT THAT INITIATES THE GREAT TERRIBLE DAY OF THE LORD! (More about the sequence of events in the next chapter.)

Acts 1: 9-11 speaks of Jesus' ascension and affirms the manner in which He will gather all believers:

> *"After he said this, he was taken up before their very eyes, and a cloud hid him from their sight. They were looking intently up into the sky as he was going, when suddenly two men dressed in white stood beside them. 'Men of Galilee', they said, 'Why do you stand here looking into the sky? This same Jesus who has been taken from you into heaven, will come back in the same way you have seen him go into heaven.'"*

Jesus speaking in Matthew 16:27

> *"For the Son of Man is going to come in his Father's glory with his angels, and then he will reward each person according to what he has done."*

In this verse, Jesus is teaching about the "first resurrection/rapture," when He will reward his followers for their faithfulness. This lines up perfectly with Paul's teaching about the "coming of the Lord" for both the "dead in Christ" and those believers who are still alive in Christ.

Paul addresses another issue in I Thessalonians 5:1-2:

> *"Now, brothers, about times and dates we do*
> *not need to write you, for you know very well*
> *that the day of the Lord will come like a thief*
> *in the night."*

It is futile to set a specific time or date for Jesus' return. The truth from Scripture is all true believers are to be ready whenever Christ returns for us.

There should not be any attempt to set limits on Almighty God by putting the restraints of time or date on Jesus' return. Many have tried and many have failed. Yet, the Lord gives His people plenty of signs and indicators of events that lead up to His coming. Paul gives several descriptions in the next several verses. In 1 Thessalonians 5:3, Paul writes,

> *"While people are saying, 'Peace and safety',*
> *destruction will come upon them suddenly, as*
> *labor pains on a pregnant woman, and they*
> *will not escape."*

Paul affirms this truth in 2 Thessalonians 1:6-10:

"God is just; He will pay back trouble to those who trouble you and give relief to you who are troubled, and to us as well. This will happen when the Lord Jesus is revealed from heaven in blazing fire with his powerful angels. He will punish those who do not know God and do not obey the Gospel of our Lord Jesus. They will be punished with everlasting destruction and shut out from the presence of the Lord and from the majesty of his power on the day he comes to be glorified in his holy people and to be marveled at among all those who have believed."

Paul encourages believers beginning in 1 Thessalonians 5:4,

"But you, brothers, are not in darkness so that this day should surprise you as a thief."

God's true followers will be ready at the time of Christ's coming. Jesus said,

"My sheep know my voice" (John 10:3).

He has sent the Holy Spirit to lead us and guide us to all truth (John 16:13). Therefore, those who are truly "born again" of the Spirit will be ready.

269

The apostle continues in verses five through eight,

"You are all sons of the light and sons of the day. We do not belong to the night or to the darkness. So then, let us not be like others, who are asleep, but let us be alert and self-controlled. For those who sleep, sleep at night, and those who get drunk, get drunk at night. But since we belong to the day, let us be self controlled, putting on faith and love as a breastplate, and the hope of salvation as a helmet."

In verse five, Paul states, *"You are sons of the light"* – God's people have always been associated with the "Light of the World"- the Lord Jesus Christ. Jesus describes his followers in Matthew 5:14, *"You are the light of the world"*. He also describes himself in John 8:12, *"I am the light of the world."* Paul reassures the Thessalonians using these same biblical analogies. Christians do not simply live in the light. As each believer loves and obeys, the light of Christ shines through their lives bringing hope to a lost and dark world.

In verse six Paul challenges his hearers, *"let us not be like others who are asleep."* By "asleep" he means spiritually dead – those who do not believe in Jesus Christ. If they do not know Him they certainly will not live in expectation of His coming! In other words – those who are spiritually dead will not be looking for Jesus' return.

The phrase, *"but let us be alert and self controlled,"* literally means to "watch and be prepared." The believer is to be spiritually and mentally alert or ready. Jesus said in Matthew 25:13, *"Therefore, keep watch, because you do not know the day or the hour."* To "keep watch" is not passive, it is an action – His followers are to take action by loving Him, praying and communing with Him, studying His word and serving Him by helping others to come into a right relationship with Him.

Contrasting this picture of faithfulness with verse seven, we see the unbeliever going through life seemingly unconcerned about living for Christ. These people, just as in the days of Noah, are going through the motions of daily living – eating, drinking, sleeping. Otherwise, living in spiritual darkness. Jesus said in Matthew 24: 37-39,

> *"As it was in the days of Noah, so it will be at the coming of the Son of Man. For in the days before the flood, people were eating and drinking, marrying and giving in marriage, up to the day Noah entered the ark; and they knew nothing about what would happen until the flood came and took them all away. That is how it will be at the coming of the Son of Man."* No wonder Paul states in Romans 1:20, *"For since the creation of the world God's*

invisible qualities – his eternal power and divine nature – have been clearly seen, being understood from what has been made, so that men are without excuse."

In verse eight we read,

"But since we belong to the day, let us be self controlled, putting on faith and love as a breastplate, and hope of salvation as a helmet."

Notice the "great triad" – faith, hope and love. As Paul teaches in I Corinthians 13:13,

"And now these three remain: faith, hope and love. But the greatest of these is love."

This faith produces Godly action. This hope is not wishful thinking but a firm, unshakable confidence in the "rock" of our salvation! This love is none other than the greatest of all loves – AGAPE. His love motivates believers to lay down our lives and to take up our cross in order for others to come to know Him.

Paul closes out this passage with powerful and encouraging truth.

"For God did not appoint us to suffer wrath but to receive salvation through our Lord Jesus Christ. He died for us so that, whether we are awake or asleep, we may live together with him. Therefore, encourage one another and build each other up, just as in fact you are doing."

Again in verse nine it says, "God did not appoint us to suffer wrath." What wrath? Paul writes in 1 Thessalonians 1:10 "...to wait for his Son from heaven, whom he raised from the dead – Jesus, who rescues us from the coming wrath." Therefore, we know "Who" rescues or saves us from the coming wrath – but still, what wrath? Paul clearly answers this question in Romans 1:18,

"the wrath of God is being revealed from heaven against all the godlessness and wickedness of men who suppress the truth by their wickedness."

Thus, God has not appointed those who believe in Christ Jesus to suffer His wrath. THIS DOES NOT MEAN BELIEVERS WILL BE EXCUSED FROM THE WRATH OF SATAN in the first part of the seven-year tribulation (Daniel 7:25, Revelation 13:7)! The truth of verse nine is simply that believers will not be on planet earth when God's wrath/judgment comes, as the first resurrection/rapture is "the" event that kicks off the "great terrible Day of the Lord!" God's wrath occurs after Satan's wrath or the forty-two month rule of antichrist (Revelation 13:5). Jesus spoke of this wrath against his saints in Luke 21:24,

> "They will fall by the sword and will be taken
> as prisoners to all the nations. Jerusalem will
> be trampled on by the Gentiles until the times
> of the Gentiles are fulfilled."

All of this is speaking of the wrath of Satan through "antichrist" – NOT God's wrath – once the "day" or time of the Gentiles is completed, Jesus comes in all of His Glory and has His angels to gather the elect from the four winds or four "corners" of the globe (Matthew 24:31).

Paul writes of Jesus in 1 Thessalonians 5:10,

> "He died for us so that whether we are awake
> or asleep, we may live together with him."

Reaffirming to the church of Thessalonica an earlier truth (4:15-16), the apostle does not want anyone to misunderstand. We can trust God with our dead loved ones, we can trust Him with our living loved ones – we can trust Christ with everything! Again, in Romans 14:9, Paul writes of the power of Jesus' resurrection,

"For this very reason, Christ died and returned to life so that he might be the Lord of both the dead and the living."

Jesus confirms this truth to John in Revelation 1:17b-18,

"Do not be afraid. I am the First and the Last. I am the Living One; I was dead, and behold I am alive forever and ever! And I hold the keys of death and Hades."

No wonder Paul says in verse eleven, (1 Thessalonians 5:11),

"Therefore, encourage one another and build each other up, just as in fact you are doing."

The word in Greek for "build" actually applies to constructing houses. Paul uses it here to help his readers see a vivid word picture as to how we, as Christians, should be edifying each other. Raising up or "building up" a structure is a tremendous application for each believer. We should not be worried about our own needs (Matthew 6:33), rather focus on "building up" or encouraging others in their relationship with Jesus. Think about it, through Jesus' life, death, resurrection and ascension – we can receive all of God's best! The Gospel simply means "Good news." Are you sharing the "Good News" with others? Are you encouraging your fellow Christians? If not, why not? We have the greatest news of all time! We should be sharing this "news" and "encouraging each other with these words" everyday.

Paul's Teaching on "The Man of Lawlessness"

The second major writing of Paul concerning the "end time" events, is found in II Thessalonians 2:1-12. In this passage the apostle describes the "antichrist" and gives us some most important facts about his rise to power. Here, I want to encourage you, as a student of God's Word, to compare Paul's teachings in 1 and 2 Thessalonians to Christ's teaching in Matthew 24. Scripture does align with scripture as Paul emphatically writes in Galatians 1: 7b-9,

> "... Evidently some people are throwing you into confusion and are trying to pervert the Gospel of Christ. But even if we, or an angel from heaven should preach a Gospel other than the one we preached to you, let him be eternally condemned! As we have already said, so now I say again: If anybody is preaching to you a Gospel other than what you accepted, let him be eternally condemned."

The apostle's "end time" teaching here, in his second letter to the Thessalonians, is in fact, the teaching from the Gospel that is straight out of the mouth of Jesus Christ.

II Thessalonians 2:1-4,

"Concerning the coming of our Lord Jesus Christ and our being gathered to him, we ask you, brothers not to become easily unsettled or alarmed by some prophecy, report or letter supposed to have come from us, saying that the day of the Lord has already come. Don't let anyone deceive you in any way for (that day will not come), until the rebellion occurs and the man of lawlessness is revealed, the man doomed to destruction. He will oppose and will exalt himself over everything that is called God or is worshipped, so that he sets himself up in God's temple, proclaiming himself to be God."

The main topic of this passage is identified in verse one, *"the coming of our Lord Jesus Christ and our being gathered to him"* (Matthew 24:31, Mark 13:27). Paul writes in verses one b - two,

"we ask you, brothers, not to become easily unsettled or alarmed by some prophecy, report or letter supposed to have come from us, saying that the day of the Lord had already come."

Thus, Paul addresses a false teaching about Jesus' coming and the "rapture." False teachers, just as Jesus prophesied in Matthew 24, had come to the Thessalonians spreading their "lies" that "the day of the Lord" had already come.

What Paul says next is vital to our understanding of the timing of the events of the "last days." Please open your mind to the Holy Spirit as Jesus said in John 16:13,

> *"But when He, the Spirit of truth, come, he will guide you into all truth. He will not speak on his own; he will speak only what he hears, and he will tell you what is yet to come."*

Therefore, the Holy Spirit will "lead us into all truth and tell us of what is yet to come." The world (unbelievers) does not understand this because they have no relationship with Jesus Christ. The Lord teaches us that truth in John 14:17,

> *"the Spirit of truth, the world cannot accept him, because it neither sees him nor knows him, But you know him, for he lives with you and will be in you."*

II Thessalonians 2:3 is key to our understanding the "timing" – NOT the time and date, but the timing of the "day of the Lord." Paul writes, "Don't let anyone deceive you in any way, [for that day will not come] until the rebellion occurs and the man of lawlessness is revealed, the man doomed to destruction." Right off the bat, Paul warns "do not let anyone deceive you in any way", which is precisely what Jesus warned in Matthew 24:4, Mark 13:5, Luke 21:8.

Look at the two things that must happen BEFORE Christ "gathers all believers" unto Himself. One, "that day will not come until the rebellion occurs." - a Rebellion or a great number of people "falling away" by renouncing their faith in Jesus. The Lord taught this truth in Matthew 24:10-12. The second thing that will occur BEFORE the rapture is the revealing of the identity of the "Man of lawlessness" – the "man of sin" – the antichrist of Revelation 13.

These two events must take place before the rapture as Paul teaches here in verse three. As stated in an earlier chapter – I have no desire to divide the body of Christ. Yet God, through His Word and Spirit, has convicted me to always consistently teach and preach the truth as found in the scripture. Therefore, I do not wish to debate concerning when the rapture will occur. You may be a proponent of a pre-tribulation rapture, a mid-tribulation rapture or a post-tribulation rapture. However, before we move ahead, allow me to ask you a vital question, "What does the Holy Word of God teach?" Please let me re-emphasize, I do not want to win you to my perspective. The Word, as we carefully compare scripture to scripture, teaches clearly and without a doubt that Jesus will "gather" or "rapture" his people AFTER two important events— First: the "great rebellion" or falling away from the Christian faith. We see this as having already begun in our day and age. As many in the mainline denominations are already leaving the scriptural teachings of Lord, motivated by their own lust. Second, the identity of the antichrist must be revealed. The Lord wants His people to be ready for His coming. We who are alive when Jesus comes will recognize this "man of sin" because the Holy Spirit will reveal this truth to us. Christians do not need to speculate or to waste time fretting over who it will be. We have God's Word and His Spirit – what more do we need?

Paul's description in 2 Thessalonians 2:4,

> "He will oppose and will exalt himself over everything that is called God or is worshipped, so that he sets himself up in God's temple proclaiming to be God."

Amazingly, this is affirmed in Matthew 24:15; Daniel 9:27, 7:21, 7:25, 11:36-45; and Revelation 13:1-10. Also, we see the description of Satan's pride, arrogance and rebellion against God in his demands to be worshipped in Isaiah 14:13-14,

> "You said in your heart, 'I will ascend to heaven; I will raise my throne above the stars of God; I will sit enthroned on the mount of assembly, on the utmost heights of the sacred mountain. I will ascend above the tops of the clouds; I will make myself like the Most High.'"

Satan's lust to be worshipped is also seen when he tempted our Lord. The scene is found in Luke 4:5-7,

> *"The devil led him up to a high place and showed him in an instant all the kingdoms of the world. And he said to him, 'I will give you all their authority and splendor, for it has been given to me, and I can give it to anyone I want to. So if you worship me, it will all be yours.'"*

In verse eight, Jesus answers,

> *"It is written: Worship the Lord your God and serve Him only"* (Deuteronomy 6:13).

In this Luke 4 passage, Jesus sets an awesome example for all of His followers. When Satan tempts – USE THE WORD! The devil came to Christ when he was at a very physically weak point (he had fasted for forty days). Yet Jesus did not fail to quote scripture against evil for the victory. This is exactly what God wants for His people – VICTORY OVER EVIL! Our heavenly Father has given us this victory and it will be accomplished through His mighty Word. Matthew 24:35,

"Heaven and earth will pass away, but my words will never pass away" (Matthew 5:18, Psalm 119:89, Isaiah 40:8).

Jesus succeeded in resisting the temptation of Satan, but "antichrist" will fail and fall. The devil said to Jesus in Luke 4,

"I can give authority of the kingdoms of earth to anyone I want to."

The "beast" will accept Satan's proposition and will prosper temporarily, BUT he will go to his ultimate doom (II Thessalonians 2:3, 2:8; Revelation 19:20, Daniel 7:26).

Paul writes in II Thessalonians 2:5-8,

"Don't you remember that when I was with you I used to tell you these things? And now you know what is holding him back, so that he may be revealed at the proper time. For the secret power of lawlessness is already at work; but the one who now holds it back will continue to do so till he is taken out of the way. And then the lawless one will be revealed, whom the Lord Jesus will overthrow with the breath of his mouth and destroy by the splendor of his coming."

In verse five, Paul reminds the Thessalonians that he previously taught them about these events when he was with them. This conversation was obviously an oral presentation as this passage is not found in any of his writings to the Thessalonians, nor is it recorded anywhere else in Scripture.

These next two verses of the passage are rather mysterious. Verses 6-7,

> *"And now you know what is holding him back, so that he may be revealed at the proper time. For the secret power of lawlessness is already at work; but the one who now holds it back will continue to do so till he is taken out of the way."*

Paul states with confidence and certainty that the events of the "Day of the Lord" will not, cannot begin until the "one holding antichrist back" is "taken out of the way." Once this restrainer of lawlessness is removed – "antichrist" will be "revealed" as the "beast" he truly is. Paul writes, "you know what is holding him (antichrist) back." The "what" in this phrase is stated in the neuter form. However, in verse seven, it is stated in the masculine ("the one who holds it back" "he will continue to do so").

Who could this "restrainer" be? This question has been hotly debated in the church for sometime. Yet, his identity DOES NOT CHANGE THE TRUTH ABOUT THE SEQUENCE OF END-TIME

EVENTS! We need to stay focused on this truth – whoever the "restrainer" is; God knows his identity and will take him out of the way to reveal "antichrist's" true intentions.

Many have said that "the one who holds antichrist back" is the Holy Spirit. Others have said it's the "true church." According to Paul's teaching in this text, "for that day (the Day of the Lord) will not come, until the rebellion occurs and the man of lawlessness is revealed," neither the Holy Spirit nor the church are viable possibilities. Again, Paul's teaching says the great "falling away" and the "antichrist's true identity" must be revealed – after these two events take place, the rapture of the "church" will take place. Therefore, the church will be here when "antichrist" is revealed which eliminates the "body of Christ" from this role of restrainer. Also, the Holy Spirit will still be on planet earth after the antichrist is revealed and begins his "war against the saints."

Others have offered suggestions concerning the identity of this powerful restrainer—the Jewish state, human government, even Paul's missionary work. Scripturally, none of these offerings are viable. Yet, the late Robert Van Kampen offers a real biblical possibility. In his book "The Rapture Question Answered," he writes, "I think a strong case can be made for the restrainer being the archangel Michael." We learn from the prophet Daniel that Michael's work is to "stand firmly against" or "restrain" the forces of evil (Daniel 10:21), and we are later told that Michael will "arise" or "stand still" (Daniel 12:1) just prior to the great persecution of antichrist. The idea in the Hebrew text is that Michael, "who stands guard over the sons of your people," must remove his protection – arise, and stand still – before "there will be a time of distress such as never occurred since there was a nation until that time " (Daniel 12:1).[1]

As Van Kampen points out, this truth from Daniel lines up perfectly with Paul's teaching in this 2 Thessalonians 2 passage. However, as I have already stated, the "identity of the restrainer does not affect the sequence of events that must occur before Christ comes. We only know that he must be removed before Antichrist can be revealed, and that Antichrist must be revealed before the events described in verse eight can occur." [2]

When the "restrainer" is taken out of the way, verse eight takes place,

> *"And then the lawless one will be revealed, whom the Lord Jesus will overthrow with the breath of his mouth and destroy by the splendor of his coming."*

Isaiah 11:4 aligns perfectly with this verse. The great prophet sees far into the future when he prophesies of Jesus' Second Coming,

> *"but with righteousness he will judge the needy, with justice he will give decisions for the poor of the earth. He will strike the earth*

with the rod of his mouth; with the breath of
his lips he will slay the wicked."

Pause here just for a moment and meditate on the awesomeness of our God. Seven hundred years before Christ's first coming, God Almighty spoke to and through the prophet Isaiah concerning the Battle of Armageddon! The Biblical reference of this truth about Jesus' coming judgment is found in Revelation 19:15,

> *"Out of his mouth comes a sharp sword with*
> *which to strike down the nations. He will rule*
> *them with an iron scepter. He treads the*
> *winepress of the jury of the wrath of God*
> *Almighty." The judgment of the antichrist in*
> *Revelation 19:20,*

> *"but the beast was captured, with him the*
> *false prophet ...The two of them were thrown*
> *alive into the fiery lake of burning sulfur."*

The biblical picture of "true" Armageddon is found in Revelation 19:11-21. With this truth, we can understand more fully what Paul meant when he described "antichrist" as "the man doomed to destruction" (2 Thess. 2-3c).

Let us now close out Paul's teaching in 2 Thessalonians 2, verses 9-12,

286

"The coming of the lawless one will be in accordance with the work of Satan displayed in all kinds of counterfeit miracles, signs and wonders, and in every sort of evil that deceives those who are perishing. They perish because they refused to love the truth and so be saved. For this reason God sent them a powerful delusion so that they will believe a lie and so that all will be condemned who have not believed the truth but have delighted in wickedness."

In verse nine, Paul points out that "antichrist's" rise to power will be a working of Satan through counterfeit signs, miracles and wonders. This is exactly what Jesus teaches in Matthew 24:24,

"For false christs and false prophets will appear and perform great signs and miracles to deceive even the elect – if that were possible."

Revelation 13:13 affirms this truth concerning the beast and his false prophets,

"And he performed great and miraculous signs, even causing fire to come down from heaven to earth in full view of men."

We know that the Holy Spirit protects His sheep, who know His voice, by leading us and guiding us to all truth (John 10:27, 15:26, 16:8). Therefore, true believers have nothing to worry about concerning Satan's or "antichrist's" deceptions – the Holy Spirit will protect us.

In verse ten, the rise of "antichrist" will also be in accordance with "every sort of evil that deceives those who are perishing." Paul even explains why they are perishing – "they refused to love the truth." All who reject God's truth as found in His Son are going to be deceived. The evil people spoken of in this verse will willingly and intentionally choose "antichrist" over the true Christ! This truth is affirmed throughout Scripture but particularly in two places. In 1 Corinthians 1:18, Paul writes,

> *"For the message of the cross is foolishness to those who are perishing, but to us who are being saved it is the power of God."*

Secondly, Jesus says in John 3:17-19,

> *"For God did not send his Son into the world to condemn the world, but to save the world through him. Whoever believes in him is not condemned, but whoever does not believe stands condemned already because he has not believed in the name of God's one and only*

Son. This is the verdict: Light has come into the world, but men loved darkness instead of light because their deeds were evil."

These two passages (1 Corinthians 1:18-31, John 3:17-19) shed abundant light on verses eleven and twelve. Paul finishes this teaching about "antichrist" and his followers with these words,

"For this reason God sends them a powerful delusion so that they will believe the lie and so that all will be condemned who have not believed the truth but have delighted in wickedness."

Make no mistake about this truth – God does not cause these people to follow Satan and "antichrist." However, because these human beings exercised their free will and chose to follow evil, "God will send them a powerful delusion." God sends them the delusion because of their deliberate rejection of Truth. They in essence say, Antichrist "will be our savior" – "we will worship Satan" (Revelation 13:4). The lie they choose to believe is NOT just any lie – but the greatest of all lies – that the "Antichrist/Beast" is God! Thus, the Lord gives them over to sin – they lusted after this leader, they wanted him more than the true God – the Father allows the law of reaping and sowing to overtake them. Paul affirms this in Romans 1:28-32,

"Furthermore, since they did not think it worthwhile to retain the knowledge of God, he gave them over to a depraved mind, to do what ought to be done. They have become filled with every kind of wickedness, evil, greed and depravity. They are full of envy, murder, strife, deceit and malice. They are gossips, slanderers, God-haters, insolent, arrogant and boastful; they invent ways of doing evil; they disobey their parents; they are senseless, faithless, heartless, ruthless. Although they know God's righteous decree that those who do such things deserve death, they not only continue to do these very things but also approve of those who practice them."

I do not know what this passage says to you, but for me, this teaching draws me to a word of encouragement and commitment. This word is found in Joshua 24:14-15. Joshua is speaking to the people of the true and living God,

"Now fear the Lord and serve him with all faithfulness. Throw away the gods your forefathers worshipped beyond the River and in Egypt, and serve the Lord. But if serving the Lord seems undesirable to you, then choose for

yourselves this day whom you will serve, whether the god your forefathers served beyond the River, or the gods of the Amorites, in whose land you are living. But as for me and my household, WE WILL SERVE THE LORD."

CHAPTER 11

BRINGING IT ALL TOGETHER

S o often we human beings tend to think of life in a linear fashion—historical timelines and datelines, when certain important events took place in the past. Today's church tends to do the same with future, prophetic, biblical teachings. I have already shared the scriptural truth - we do not know the date nor hour when Jesus will return (Matthew 24:42). However, searching and researching the truth through God's Word and comparing scripture with scripture, we can see the aligning of the events. I want to encourage you again to open your mind and heart to the Holy Spirit as He reveals His truth of the return of Jesus Christ.

With that being said, we now need to shift our focus. Mainly from a timeline and dateline mentality to the biblical truth we will discover in this chapter's discussion of the "end time event line" as it pertains to Daniel's 70th week. We will look at the timing of ten major events of the "Great Seven Year Tribulation" as it relates to the close of the age. First, let's look at several precursors that set the stage for the final seven years of sin's rule on planet earth.

Vital Precursors

As stated in an earlier chapter, the year 1948 was a most significant year in setting the stage for end-time prophecies and the appearance of the "man of lawlessness" (2 Thessalonians 2:3). The "key" occurrences of this year include: Israel regained statehood; the introduction of a united Europe; the formation of the World Council of Churches; the invention of the tiny transistor which opened the technological door for our current computers (Jon Courson, Searchlight Ministries).

These important factors contribute to a world scene that would be conducive to a "one-world" leader. Not only does Israel need to be a nation, she also must control Jerusalem, which occurred in 1967. The uniting of Europe (Daniel 7:23-24a) is the revived Roman Empire from which the "Antichrist" will come. The founding of the World Council of Churches lends itself to a possible rise to the power of the false prophet of Revelation thirteen. The invention of the transistor was the doorway to computer technology that has ushered in the new age of an unprecedented world economy. Transactions can be and are being made from anywhere on the globe through the Internet.

Also, dovetailing with these amazing events is the rise of the false religions, cults and the revival of Islam. Just think about it, since about 1830 with Joseph Smith's claims, there have been scores of false teachings to come upon the scene. Mormonism, Jehovah's Witness (1879), The Way International, The World Wide Church of God, Christian Science – just to name a few. Then we have godless world philosophies – Marxism, Socialism, Secular Humanism, Atheism and Agnosticism. And finally the major world religions of

Buddhism, Hinduism, Judaism and Islam all claim to have the "truth" – BUT NONE of them knowing the Truth as they all have varying degrees of bondage. Jesus said in John 8:31-32,

"If you hold to my teaching, you are really my disciples. Then you will know the truth, and the truth will set you free."

Just look around you, the world is presently witnessing the convergence of all the things Jesus spoke of in Matthew twenty-four:

> *"Wars, rumors of wars, nation will rise up against nation, and kingdom against kingdom"* (Matthew 24:6-7).

Consider the rise of China, the nuclear threat of North Korea and Iran, the absolute stunning growth of terrorism and Russia still lurking in the background. The failed policies of the United Nations are many times anti-Israel, anti American and anti-God. One does not have to be a Bible scholar to see that some very unusual things are taking place.

Also, we are witnessing a rise in the occult - fortunetellers, psychics, necromancy, astrology, UFO's – even worship of Satan. As Jesus said, "we should not be alarmed." Paul writes in 1 Timothy 4:1:

> *"The Spirit clearly says that in later times some will abandon the faith and follow deceiving spirits and things taught by demons"* (Matthew 24:10-12).

295

Paul confirms this truth again in 2 Timothy 3:1-5,

> *"But mark this: There will be terrible times in the last days. People will be lovers of themselves, lovers of money, boastful, proud, abusive, disobedient to their parents, ungrateful, unholy, brutal, not lovers of the good, treacherous, rash, conceited, lovers of pleasure rather than lovers of God – having a form of godliness but denying its power. Have nothing to do with them."*

The apostle wrote that to a young pastor almost twenty centuries ago, and yet it is almost as if Paul was reporting today's news and headlines.

With all of these terrible things happening simultaneously, isn't it awesome to hear the calm, still, loving, peaceful voice of Jesus saying,

> *"... but see to it that you are not alarmed. Such things must happen, but the end is still to come"* (Matthew 24:6b).

Let us now focus our attention on the ten major events of the close of Satan's reign over planet earth. I encourage you with all of my heart; listen to the warning given by Jesus, *"Watch out that no one deceives you"* (Matthew 24:4, Mark 13:5, Luke 21:8).

Drawing Back the Curtain

We know from Jesus' teaching in Matthew 24:21-22, that this time, at least part of it, will hold "unequalled distress." Christ's words in this passage are very intense,

> *"For then there will be a great distress, unequaled from the beginning of the world until now – and never to be equaled again. If those days had not been cut short, no one would survive, but for the sake of the elect those days will be shortened."*

This seven-year period of "unequaled distress" is cut short for the believer by Jesus' coming. We see this in Matthew 24:29-31,

> *"<u>Immediately</u> after the distress of those days, 'the sun will be darkened, and the moon will not give its light; the stars will fall from the sky, and the heavenly bodies will be shaken'. <u>At that time</u> the sign of the Son of Man will appear in the sky, and all the nations of the earth will mourn. They will see the Son of Man coming on the clouds of the sky, with power and great glory. And he will send his angels with a loud trumpet call, and they will gather his elect from the four winds, from one end of*

the heavens to the other" (author emphasis
added).

Therefore, the "tribulation" period IS NOT STARTED BY THE RAPTURE! This teaching of a rapture that happens before the seven-year tribulation CANNOT BE SUPPORTED when the Bible student compares scripture to scripture! The gathering of the elect is when Jesus removes all believers from the hands of Antichrist – "immediately *after* the distress" (Matthew 24:29).

Also, when we take the time to compare scripture with scripture, we will clearly see that the Battle of Armageddon <u>DOES NOT</u> open the Tribulation period. It amazes me to see so many movies, news magazines, T.V. and radio talk shows – all espousing or depicting their opinions and views of "Armageddon." Tragically, most of these I have seen do not even think to look in the one place for the right (truthful) answers! God's Word supplies us with all we need to know – the Battle of Armageddon found in Revelation chapters fourteen and nineteen, teach clearly that this great battle closes this time of "unequalled distress."

If neither the "Rapture" nor the "Battle of Armageddon" opens the "Great Tribulation" – what does? Lets go to Daniel 9:27,

> *"He will confirm a covenant with many for one*
> *'seven'. In the middle of the seven he will put*
> *an end to sacrifice and offering. And on the*
> *wing of the temple, he will set up an*

abomination that causes desolation, until the
end that is decreed is poured out on him."

Some have erroneously thought that the "He" of this verse is Jesus Christ. The problem with that opinion is that it does not fit – period. Jesus did not confirm a covenant for any timeframe much less seven years. His covenant is everlasting! Our Lord and Savior did put an end to the "old way" of atonement. However, it was NOT in the middle of any seven or any time period. Jesus is God; therefore He could NOT and would NOT set up any abomination on the "temple" grounds or anywhere else in the universe. Jesus is Eternal – there will be no "end poured out on Him!" Isaiah says of Christ in Isaiah 9:6-7,

> *"For to us a child is born, to us a son is given,*
> *and the government will be on his shoulders.*
> *And he will be called Wonderful Counselor,*
> *Mighty God, Everlasting Father, Prince of*
> *Peace. Of the increase of his government and*
> *peace there will be no end. He will reign on*
> *David's throne and over his kingdom,*
> *establishing and upholding it with justice and*
> *righteousness from that time on and forever.*
> *The zeal of the Lord Almighty will accomplish*
> *this."*

Jesus, in Matthew 24:15, warns His followers about the "man of lawlessness" (2 Thessalonians 2:3). He spoke these words,

> *"So when you see standing in the holy place the 'abomination that causes desolation', spoken of through the prophet Daniel – let the reader understand."*

Let the reader understand – for anyone to teach that the person mentioned in Daniel 9:27 is Jesus Christ – this is nothing short of HERESY! Again, why would Jesus warn his followers about Himself? Obviously, this teaching makes no "Biblical" sense – it is not supported by Scripture.

However, this false teaching plays into the hands of Satan, the "Antichrist" and the false prophet. Even today, as we continue to see unprecedented conflict in the Middle East and around the globe – today's world scene begs for one to step out of the background and bring "world peace." The Orthodox Jew desiring to return to their sacrificial system of worship; the European Union, U.S. and Japan wanting peace for economic reasons; China, North Korea, Russia, Iran wanting nuclear superiority; the Muslim extremist desiring to get rid of all infidels. The timing will be perfect – for it will be God's perfect timing as He allows this possibly "unknown" man to essentially come out of "nowhere" to broker a "covenant or agreement with many."

This "peace pact" will seemingly answer all the world's great issues at once. Yet, the true believer in Christ will be able to see through it and realize the Truth. This covenant is nothing more than a counterfeit – just as Satan is a counterfeit. Isaiah, writing two hundred years before Daniel, speaks of the "peace treaty" in Isaiah 28:14-18,

> *"Therefore, hear the word of the Lord, you scoffers who rule this people in Jerusalem. You boast, 'We have entered into covenant with death, with the grave we have made an agreement. When an overwhelming scourge sweeps by, it cannot touch us, for we have made a lie our refuge and falsehood our hiding place'. So this is what the Sovereign Lord says: "See, I lay a stone in Zion, a tested stone, a precious cornerstone for a sure foundation; the one who trusts will never be dismayed. I will make justice the measuring line and righteousness the plumb line; hail will sweep away your refuge, the lie, and water will overflow your hiding place. Your covenant with death will be annulled; your agreement with the grave will not stand. When the overwhelming scourge sweeps by, you will be*

beaten down by it" (Isaiah 63:18, Daniel 8:13).

The "cornerstone" is none other than Jesus Christ. All who trust in Him will never be put to shame. However, all who choose another way of "peace" will not stand in the "Day of Judgment." All of those who sign this "covenant" of death with "antichrist" will soon receive the "mark of the beast" (Revelation 13:16) and their eternal doom (Revelation 13:8, 20:15).

This "covenant with many" is most certainly a counterfeit. This agreement/treaty is for a seven-year period. It allows the "Antichrist" time to set himself up as God (2 Thessalonians 2:4, Matthew 24:15, Daniel 9:27). This so-called "peace pact" is more accurately – the "covenant with death that opens the great 'Seven Year Tribulation.'"

Birth Pangs

The miracle of birth -- Isn't it interesting that Jesus chose this real life experience to teach us about His miraculous second coming? What is His point? What is He saying to us? It is as plain and simple as – well – as birth. Having three great kids – my wife and I have been blessed by this experience of birth – on three separate occasions. By no means am I saying we know all there is to know about childbirth. Yet, God has taught us many truths through the "arrival" of our children. In Matthew 24:5-8, Jesus begins His response to the disciples' twofold question in verse three,

"What will be the sign of your coming and of the end of the age?" He begins, *"For many will come in my name, claiming I am the Christ, and will deceive many. You will hear of wars and rumors of wars, but see to it that you are not alarmed. Such things must happen, but the end is still to come. Nation will rise against nation, and kingdom against kingdom. There will be famines and earthquakes in various places. All these are the beginning of birth pains."*

Verse eight is the key verse – ALL THESE ARE THE BEGINNING OF BIRTH PAINS! These things Jesus speaks of happening individually do not necessarily mean anything. HOWEVER, when all are happening simultaneously – with increase in number and intensity, Jesus said, "This is the beginning of birth pains."

Staying focused on the disciples' question and then Jesus' answer becomes easier to understand. The question was about His second coming and the end of the age. Jesus uses the analogy of birth pains. Birth pains do not begin with conception. A woman has a few biological signs to let her know something is different within her body. She goes to the doctor to have tests run. The confirmation returns – she is going to have a baby. She and her husband wait patiently – taking care of her body and her baby for forty weeks. The time for baby's arrival or birth draws close. Contractions may start several minutes apart – they then happen with greater intensity and closer together. The mother's body goes through intense change and tremendous pain. The closer the contractions, the closer the baby's arrival. The pain intensifies to an almost unbearable level – then, finally, thank God, the baby is born.

If you will seriously study Matthew twenty-four and compare scripture with scripture – that is what Jesus is teaching. His second coming will be like a woman giving birth. The early signs - events happening separately of each other. The closer we get to His Coming – the events line up and begin to happen all at the same time with the intensity increasing! The contractions of the signs of world events continue until we think we cannot withstand anymore and then "the baby is born" –Jesus gathers His followers, His "true children" from the four corners of the earth!

Let's look over in Revelation 6:1-8 for clarity. This passage concerns the seals opened only by Jesus the Lamb. Observe, as each seal is opened how the intensity increases. The first seal is in Revelation 6:1-2:

> *"I watched as the Lamb opened the first of the seven seals. Then I heard one of the four living creatures say in a voice like thunder, 'Come'. I looked, and there before me was a white*

horse. Its rider held a bow, and he was given a
crown and he rode out as a conqueror bent on
conquest."

This first seal reveals a rider on a white horse. This rider is the "spirit of conquest". Mankind's sin nature is "bent on conquest", warring and fighting against each other, "nation against nation, kingdom against kingdom." Jesus Christ has already explained this in Matthew 24:7. The opening of the first seal is a comforting word from God saying, "No matter how horrible things on earth appear – I will have the victory."

Things begin to worsen with the opening of the second seal,

"When the Lamb opened the second seal, I
heard the second living creature say, "Come!"
Then another horse came out, a fiery red one.
Its rider was given power to take peace from
the earth and to make men slay each other. To
him was given a large sword" (Revelation 6:3-
4).

This red horse goes perfectly with "wars, rumors of wars, and nation rise against nation" that Jesus speaks of in Matthew 24:6-7. Divine judgment is coming, but this seems to be the "Antichrist" making war against the saints (Daniel 7:21, Revelation 13:7).

When the third seal is opened, the world's economy begins to crumble. Revelation 6:5-6 says,

"When the Lamb opened the third seal, I heard the third living creature say, "Come!" I looked, and there before me was a black horse! Its rider was holding a pair of scales in his hand. Then I heard what sounded like a voice among the four living creatures, saying, 'a quart of wheat for a day's wages, and three quarts of barley for a day's wages, and do not damage the oil and the wine."

This black horse symbolizes famine which fits perfectly with Matthew 24:7. This opened seal reveals the over-inflated prices of bread – one of our daily staples. The wars of the second seal thus causing the famines, which cause prices to be at least ten times their normal levels. This rider on the black horse is instructed by the "voice among the four living creatures", "do not damage the oil and the wine". Therefore, this famine does not bring complete destruction.

In Revelation 6:7-8,

"When the Lamb opened the fourth seal, I heard the voice of the fourth living creature say, "Come"! I looked, and there before me was

a pale horse! Its rider was named Death, and Hades was following close behind him. They were given power over a fourth of the earth to kill by sword, famine and plague, and by the wild beasts of the earth".

This pale horse of "death" is a result of "wars, nations and kingdoms rising against each other, famines and earthquakes". The instruction Jesus gives in Matthew 24 is the same instruction Jesus as the Lamb reveals as He opens the seals of the scroll described in Revelation 5:1. So far we have four seals opened and NO RAPTURE! It is only the beginning of birth pains.

Antichrist Revealed

Paul writes in 2 Thessalonians 2:1-3,

"Concerning the coming of our Lord Jesus Christ and our being gathered to him, we ask you, brothers, not to become easily unsettled or alarmed by some prophecy, report or letter supposed to have come from us, saying that the day of the Lord has already come. Don't let anyone deceive you in any way for that day will not come until the rebellion occurs and the man of lawlessness is revealed, the man doomed to destruction".

From this passage, we see total agreement and unity with Matthew 24 and Revelation 6. The "Antichrist" MUST BE REVEALED before the "Rapture" or "Resurrection Day" occurs. The great rebellion in Matthew 24: 10-11 and "the man of sin or lawlessness" in Matthew 24:15 - BOTH OF THESE EVENTS MUST TAKE PLACE BEFORE "the coming of our Lord Jesus Christ and our being gathered to him".

"Antichrist" opens the "Tribulation" with his "covenant with many" in Daniel 9:27a. Yet, this does not necessarily teach that this signing of a covenant reveals the identity of the "beast". It is when he breaks this "agreement" that his true identity is revealed! In Daniel 9:27a the treaty is signed, in the second and third parts of this verse "Antichrist's" true intentions are open for all to see. This verse reads,

> "In the middle of the seven he will put an end
> to sacrifice and offering. And on a wing of the
> temple he will set up an abomination that
> causes desolation, until the end that is decreed
> is poured out on him."

This seven-year agreement is broken in the middle – about 3 ½ years by "putting an end to sacrifice and offering." Why is it broken? Because this evil "beast" is now ready to demand worship from the whole world! Paul describes him well in 2 Thessalonians 2:4,

"He will oppose and will exalt himself over everything that is called God or is worshipped, so that he sets himself up in God's temple proclaiming himself to be God."

At this point in the 'Tribulation" period, the "Antichrist" has had enough with the world's religions. He is then prepared to demand worship from all of earth's population. Jesus warned His followers in Matthew 24:15-16,

"So when you see standing in the holy place 'the abomination that causes desolation', spoken of through the prophet Daniel – let the reader understand – then let those who are in Judea flee to the mountains."

In the next several verses Jesus warns with phrases like "flee, don't even go back into the house for your belongings, don't even go back to look for your coat" (Matthew 24:17-18).

At this point, everyone on planet earth will know the identity of "Antichrist". Many will embrace him – even worship him. However, God's true people will not! Daniel 11:31-32,

"His armed forces will rise up to desecrate the temple fortress and will abolish the daily sacrifice. Then they will set up the abomination that causes desolation. With

*flattery he will corrupt those who have
violated the covenant, but the people who
know their God will firmly resist him."*

You may still ask, "How can God's people truly know that this horrible person is the real "Antichrist"? Let's look to the Apostle John for help. Revelation thirteen confirms the teachings of Jesus, Paul and the prophecy of Daniel. John writes concerning the revealing of antichrist in Revelation 13:1-2,

*"And I saw a beast coming out of the sea. He
had ten horns and seven heads, with ten
crowns on his horns, and on each head a
blasphemous name. The beast I saw resembled
a leopard, but had feet like those of a bear and
a mouth like that of a lion. The dragon gave
the beast his power and his throne and great
authority."*

This perfectly aligns with Daniel chapter seven!

The first clue to the identification of this beast is that he comes from the masses or "sea" of peoples. The sea here represents all human beings on the earth. This "revelation" becomes more specific as this leader comes from the "revived" Roman Empire (Daniel 7:23-25). Satan gives the "beast" his "power, throne and authority." In others words, Satan selects his man from virtual obscurity in the revived Roman Empire which relates to the present day European Union.

Second identification is found in Revelation 13:3-4,

> *"One of the heads of the beast seemed to have a fatal wound, but the wound had been healed. The whole world was astonished and followed the beast. Men worshipped the dragon because he had given authority to the beast, and they also worshipped the beast and asked, Who is like the beast? Who can make war against him?"*

Make no mistake about the beast/antichrist – he will not act alone. Satan will raise up many, including the false prophet – to give antichrist success in all that he does. Satan even raises this "beast" from the dead (fatal wound – verse three). After that miracle – everyone will be able to identify "Antichrist." This is why Jesus says: "do not be deceived." This leader is going to be amazingly powerful – "Who is like the beast?"

The third clue is this "beast" has a close "right hand man." Revelation 13:11-15,

> *"Then I saw another beast, coming out of the earth. He had two horns like a lamb, but he spoke like a dragon. He exercised all the*

311

authority of the first beast on his behalf, and made the earth and its inhabitants worship the first beast, whose fatal wound had been healed. And he performed great and miraculous signs, even causing fire to come down from heaven to earth in full view of men. Because of the signs he was given power to do on behalf of the first beast, he deceived the inhabitants of the earth. He ordered them to set up an image in honor of the beast who was wounded by the sword and yet lived. He was given power to give breath to the image of the first beast, so that it could speak and cause all who refused to worship the image to be killed."

This false religious leader "seizes the opportunity" when the first beast was fatally wounded. Satan raises this "false prophet" to do counterfeit miracles, to deceive millions to give breath to the image. This liar, "who speaks like a dragon" goes so far as to "force everyone, small and great, rich and poor, free and slave, to receive a mark on his right hand or his forehead, so that no one could buy or sell unless he had the mark, which is the name of the beast or the number of his name (Revelation 13:16-17).

We can clearly identify Antichrist through God's Word. We can clearly understand that Satan is the one manipulating peoples, places and things to set up his world ruler. Look at the evidence: Satan uses the beast and false prophet to gain seemingly total control of the world economy, world government and world religion! Key word here is *seemingly*! Daniel 11:36 speaks clearly to this point,

> *"The king will do as he pleases. He will exalt and magnify himself above every god and will say unheard of things against the God of gods. He will be successful until the time of wrath is completed, for what has been determined must take place."*

Paul confirms the revealing of "Antichrist" in 2 Thessalonians 2:9-12,

> *"The coming of the lawless one will be accordance with the work of Satan displayed in all kinds of counterfeit miracles, signs and wonders, and in every sort of evil that deceives those who are perishing. They perish because they refused to love the truth and so be saved. For this reason God sends them a powerful delusion so that they will believe the lie and so*

that all will be condemned who have not believed the truth but have delighted in wickedness."

At this point in the tribulation, things are going to get worse before they get better, even for believers.

The Persecution

As Antichrist's true identity is revealed – he begins to "ratchet" up or intensify his persecution of believers – all those who refuse to receive his "mark." Jesus spoke of this horrible period in Matthew 24:9-12,

> *"Then you will be handed over to be persecuted and put to death, and you will be hated by all nations because of me. At that time many will turn away from the faith and will betray and hate each other, and many false prophets will appear and deceive many people. Because of the increase of wickedness, the love of most will grow cold."*

Who is Jesus speaking of? His true followers!

Examining the scriptures, we see a most difficult time. We must stay focused on Jesus and help others to see the "Truth". We, as believers, must remember when anyone cuts a deal with Satan – that person will pay and pay dearly! Look at the Biblical picture, "Antichrist", in the middle of the seven year period, breaks his word by putting an end to the Jewish "sacrifice and offering". Then he begins a campaign to force the entire world to worship him – by any and all means. The false prophet sends false teachers to deceive many, the entire world is forced to receive the mark or die. Jesus says of this dark time in human or church history,

> *"For then there will be great distress, unequaled from the beginning of the world until now – and never to be equaled again"* (Matthew 24:21).

Again, we witness perfect alignment in God's Word! In Daniel 7:19-25, the prophet writes

> *"Then I wanted to know the true meaning of the fourth beast, which was different from all the others and most terrifying, with its iron teeth and bronze claws – the beast that crushed and devoured its victims and trampled underfoot what was left. I also wanted to know about the ten horns on its head and about the other horn that came up, before which three of them fell – the horn that looked more imposing than the others and*

315

that had eyes and a mouth that spoke boastfully. As I watched, this horn was waging war against the saints and defeating them, until the Ancient of Days came and pronounced judgment in favor of the saints of the most High, and the time came when they possessed the kingdom. He gave me this explanation: the fourth beast is a fourth kingdom that will appear on earth. It will be different from all the other kingdoms and will devour the whole earth, trampling it down and crushing it. The ten horns are ten kings who will come from this kingdom. After them another king will arise, different from the earlier ones; he will subdue three kings. He will speak against the Most High and oppress his saints and try to change the set times and the laws. The saints will be handed over to him for a time, times and half a time (or three and a half years)".

Looking at this perfect description of Antichrist's persecution of the saints – I CANNOT FOR THE LIFE OF ME understand why anyone would believe or teach a "Pre-Tribulation" rapture.

If God only gave us the Daniel 7:19-25 passage – that should be enough! But he didn't! Let's go back to Revelation thirteen, and look at John's description of the beast, his actions against God and His people. In verses 5-8,

> *"The beast was given a mouth to utter proud words and blasphemies and to exercise his authority for forty-two months. He opened his mouth to blaspheme God, and to slander his name and his dwelling place and those who live in heaven. He was given power to make war against the saints and to conquer them. And he was given authority over every tribe, people, language and nation. All inhabitants of the earth will worship the beast – all whose names have not been written in the Book of Life belonging to the Lamb that was slain from the creation of the world."*

Dark days and dark times are upon us and it seems to continue to get worse. Remember Revelation six? We have only opened four seals. Let's examine verses 9-11 as Jesus opens the fifth seal:

> *"When he opened the fifth seal, I saw under the altar the souls of those who had been slain*

because of the word of God and the testimony they had maintained. They called out in a loud voice, 'How long, Sovereign Lord, holy and true, until you judge the inhabitants of the earth and avenge our blood?' Then each of them was given a white robe, and they were told to wait a little longer, until the number of their fellow servants and brothers who were to be killed as they had been was completed."

These true believers refused the "mark of the beast", refused to bow down and worship "antichrist" and it cost them their very lives! Yet – praise God – they will live and reign with Christ forever (Revelation 20:4-6)! These faithful servants were "told to wait a little longer" – be patient for God's deliverance! Also, we have five seals opened and NO RAPTURE! "Wait a little longer" is the key. This wonderful hope is found in Daniel 12:1,

"At that time Michael, the great prince who protects your people, will arise. There will be a time of distress such as has not happened from the beginning of nations until then. But at that time your people – everyone whose name is found written in the book – will be delivered" (Matthew 24: 29-31, 1 Thessalonians 4:13-18, Revelation 7:9-17). As dark as this

318

unequaled distress will be – in Christ there is
a perfect hope!

The Gathering

When is the timing of the "rapture"? Where does it fit in the
"seven-year tribulation period"? Jesus answers in Matthew 24:29-
31,

> *"Immediately after the distress of those days,*
> *the sun will be darkened, and the moon will*
> *not give its light; the stars will fall from the*
> *sky, and the heavenly bodies will be shaken. At*
> *that time the sign of the Son of Man will*
> *appear in the sky, and all the nations of the*
> *earth will mourn. They will see the Son of Man*
> *coming on the clouds of the sky, with power*
> *and great glory. And he will send his angels*
> *with a loud trumpet call, and they will gather*
> *his elect from the four winds, from one end of*
> *the heavens to the other."*

Does John agree? Let's go back to Revelation six and examine
the opening of the sixth seal. John writes in verses 12-14,

> *"I watched as he opened the sixth seal. There*
> *was a great earthquake. The sun turned black*

like sackcloth made of goat hair, the whole moon turned blood red, and the stars in the sky fell to earth, as late figs drop from a fig tree when shaken by a strong wind. The sky receded like a scroll, rolling up, and every mountain and island was removed from its place."

Paul confirms this truth in I Thessalonians 4:14-18. He also explains this further in I Corinthians 15:50-57. The apostle covers the timing question in II Thessalonians 2:1-3. In fact, Paul is the New Testament writer who, in these passages, helps us understand the "rapture" as the great "Resurrection Day" – when all believers will receive the "resurrected" or "glorified" bodies. Daniel 12:2-3 aligns with this truth,

"Multitudes who sleep in the dust of the earth will awake: some to everlasting life, others to shame and everlasting contempt. Those who are wise will shine like the brightness of the heavens, and those who led many to righteousness, like the stars for ever and ever."

Isaiah describes this awesome event in words that are almost identical to those used by Jesus, John, Paul and Daniel. Isaiah 24:18b-23,

"The floodgates of the heavens are opened, the foundations of the earth shake. The earth is broken up, the earth is split asunder, and the earth is thoroughly shaken. The earth reels like a drunkard, it sways like a hut in the wind; so heavy upon it is the guilt of its rebellion that it falls – never to rise again. In that day the Lord will punish the powers in the heavens above and the kings on the earth below. They will be herded together like prisoners bound in a dungeon; they will be shut up in prison and be punished after many days. The moon will be abased, the sun ashamed; for the Lord Almighty will reign on Mount Zion and in Jerusalem, and before its elders gloriously" (Amos 5:19, Malachi 4:1-3).

On this great "Day" God brings His deliverance to His people while beginning His holy judgment on all the wicked inhabitants of earth. Daniel described "Resurrection Day" as the day that begins the earthly reign of Jesus Christ! Daniel 7:13-14,

"In my vision at night I looked, and there before me was one like a son of man, coming with the clouds of heaven. He approached the Ancient of Days and was led into His presence.

He was given authority, glory and sovereign power; all peoples, nations and men of every language worshipped him. His dominion is an everlasting dominion that will not pass away, and his kingdom is one that will never be destroyed."

As Peter teaches in 2 Peter 3:1-10, scoffers presently have the freedom to doubt, deny and even reject the truth about Jesus Christ's coming. However, all authority has been given to the Son of Man (Matthew 28:18); and He will rule and reign as King of kings and Lord of lords to the glory of God the Father (Philippians 2:9-11, 1 Timothy 6:15, Revelation 17:14, 19:16).

Let us now turn our attention to the scene in heaven on "Resurrection Day" when all of God's saints will be gathered unto Him. This truth is revealed in Revelation 7:9-17. Notice the first part of Revelation chapter seven, we see the 144,000 servants – 12,000 from each tribe of Israel – being sealed. Then beginning in verse nine, John writes,

"After this I looked and there before me was a great multitude that no one could count, from every nation, tribe, people and language, standing before the throne and in front of the Lamb. They were wearing white robes and were holding palm branches in their hands.

And they cried out in a loud voice: 'Salvation belongs to our God, who sits on the throne, and to the Lamb'. All the angels were standing around the throne and around the elders and the four living creatures. They fell down on their faces before the throne and worshipped God, saying: 'Amen! Praise and glory and wisdom and thanks and honor and power, and strength be to our God for ever and ever. Amen!' Then one of the elders asked me, 'These in white robes –who are they, and where did they come from?' I answered, 'Sir, you know'. And he said, 'These are they who have come out of the great tribulation; they have washed their robes and made them white in the blood of the Lamb. Therefore, they are before the throne of God and serve him day and night in his temple; and he who sits on the throne will spread his tent over them. Never again will they hunger; never again will they thirst. The sun will not beat upon them, nor any scorching heat. For the Lamb at the center of the throne will be their shepherd; he will lead them to springs of living water. And God will wipe away ever tear from their eyes."

What an awesome, grace-filled God and Savior!

While this scene in heaven is one of indescribable joy, exuberant fellowship, never-before-experienced worship – love flowing from God and the Lamb to the saints and from the saints to the Father, Son and Holy Spirit, the scene on planet earth is much different. God has sealed the 144,000 servants to go share His Gospel with any and all who will believe. Yet, Satan, "antichrist", the false prophet and those who received the "mark of the beast" will now begin to receive the Wrath of God. Psalm 2:9 says of the Messiah,

> *"you will rule them with an iron scepter; you will dash them to pieces like pottery."*

Jesus Himself quotes that verse in Revelation 2:27. John writes of Jesus in Revelation 19:15,

> *"Out of his mouth comes a sharp sword with which to strike down the nations. He will rule them with an iron scepter. He treads the winepress of the fury of the wrath of God Almighty."* Maybe this is why Jesus said of His coming – *"All the nations of the earth will mourn"* (Matthew 24:30).

Payday

Let's look at the two scenes that are taking place simultaneously. One – the scene on planet earth is where God's judgment is falling on the rebellious wicked who have rejected the grace offering or Atonement of Jesus Christ. Two – the scene in heaven is where God is rewarding His true and faithful followers with His riches in glory (John 14:4, II Corinthians. 5:10). Jesus warned in Matthew 6:19-21,

> *"Do not store up for yourselves treasures on earth, where moth and rust destroy, and where thieves break in and steal. But store up for yourselves treasures in heaven, where moth and rust do not destroy, and where thieves do not break in and steal. For where your treasure is, there your heart will be also."*

More on the timing of these rewards in a moment, but first let's examine what is taking place on planet earth.

Let's return to Revelation chapter six. In verses 12-14 the sixth seal is broken and we see the same signs Jesus gave concerning His Second Coming in Matthew 24: 29-31. Thus, the "rapture" or "gathering of the saints" – this event opens the Great Terrible Day of God's Judgment. We see perfect agreement in verses fifteen through seventeen of Revelation six. John writes,

*"Then the kings of the earth, the princes, the
generals, the rich, the mighty, and every slave
and every free man hid in caves and among
the rocks of the mountains. They called to the
mountains and rocks, 'Fall on us, and hide us
from the face of him who sits on the throne
and from the wrath of the Lamb!' For the
great day of their wrath has come, and who
can stand?"*

Therefore, the sixth seal is when the "rapture" takes place and initiates God's judgment upon all unbelievers.

Now let's move to Revelation eight for the opening of the seventh and final seal. This event begins the full fury of God's Wrath (Revelation 14:19), which will culminate with the Battle of Armageddon. But first, Revelation 8:1-5:

*"When he opened the seventh seal, there was
silence in heaven for about half an hour. And I
saw the seven angels who stand before God,
and to them were given seven trumpets.
Another angel, who had a golden censer, came
and stood at the altar. He was given much
incense to offer, with the prayers of all the
saints, on the golden altar before the throne.
The smoke of the incense, together with the*

prayers of the saints, went up before God from the angel's hand. Then the angel took the censer, filled it with fire from the altar, and hurled it on the earth; and there came peals of thunder, rumblings, flashes of lightning and an earthquake."

Judgment day has arrived!

This seventh seal is a vital transition point – from the seven seals to the seven trumpets. We witness the first six trumpets and their doom in Revelation 8:6 – 9:21 (We will view the seventh seal in the scene taking place in heaven). These first six trumpets announce an increasing flow of God's Wrath – hail; fire mixed with blood; a fiery meteorite landing in the sea; a great blazing stone ruining the fresh waters of earth; darkening of one third of the sun, moon and stars; smoke coming out of the abyss; stinging scorpions; and the 200 million demonic "horsemen" sent to kill a third of mankind. With all of this taking place on earth – amazingly the

"rest of mankind that were not killed by these plagues still did not repent of the work of their hands; they did not stop worshipping demons, and idols of gold, silver, bronze, stone and wood – idols that cannot see or hear or walk. Nor did they repent of their murders their

magic arts, their sexual immorality or their thefts" (Revelation 9:20-21).

Though hard to imagine, conditions on earth worsen. Revelation 15:1 announces the last seven plagues or "bowls" that will complete God's wrath. Revelation 16:2 tells us that these judgments are directed at "the people who had the mark of the beast and worshipped his image." The entire chapter of Revelation 16 is devoted to the horrible, ghastly description of these seven plagues/bowls poured out on the unbelieving world population.

While all of God's judgment is being poured out on earth – the picture in heaven is quite different.

We will now examine the seventh trumpet. The time for rewarding the faithful has come. John describes this event in heaven in Revelation 11:15-19,

> *"The seventh angel sounded his trumpet, and there were loud voices in heaven, which said, 'The kingdom of the world has become the kingdom of our Lord and his Christ, and He will reign for ever and ever." And the twenty-four elders, who were seated on their thrones before God, fell on their faces and worshipped God, saying 'We give thanks to you, Lord God Almighty, the One who is and who was, because you have taken your great power and*

*have begun to reign. The nations were angry;
and your wrath has come. The time has come
for judging the dead, and for rewarding your
servants, the prophets and your saints and
those who reverence your name, both small
and great – and for destroying those who
destroy the earth.' Then God's temple in
heaven was opened, and within his temple was
seen the Ark of the Covenant. And there came
flashes of lightning, rumblings, peals of
thunder, an earthquake and a great
hailstorm."*

The Ark of the Covenant in verse nineteen is significant because it represents the presence of God among his people. Also, in New Testament writings it is a symbol of God's faithfulness in keeping His promise or covenant with His people. The lightning, thunder, earthquake and hailstorm are symbols of God's awesome majesty and power. These are images of the God of the Old Covenant coming in might and power to free His New-Covenant people.

I have already documented enough about "God's wrath coming against the angry nations." The time for judging the dead which was asked about in Revelation 6:10, will be completed in Revelation 20:11-15. As for rewarding your servants (prophets, saints, everyone who reverences His Name) this is confirmed in Daniel 12:1b-3,

> *"There will be a time of distress such as has not happened from the beginning of nations until then. But at that time your people – everyone whose name is found written in the book – will be delivered. Multitudes who sleep in the dust of the earth will awake: some to everlasting life, others to shame and everlasting contempt. Those who are wise will shine like the brightness of the heavens, and those who lead many to righteousness, like the stars for ever and ever." In I Corinthians 2:9a, Paul applies Isaiah 64:4, "However, as it is written: 'No eye has seen, no ear has heard, no mind has conceived what God has prepared for those who love him."*

We cannot even fathom all of the wonderful rewards God has for those who are faithful. All the scripture verses and passages on this subject are too numerous to mention. We simply need to trust that our God will reward his true followers just as He has said. Let's be sure that we work tirelessly for Christ's Kingdom, that "we are wise and lead many to righteousness."

The Battle of Armageddon

The next great event that takes place on God's prophetic calendar is the battle that closes out His Judgment of the wicked on planet earth. As stated earlier, much is written about this subject in the "secular media"—movies, magazine articles, books, television talk shows, etc. Yet, the Bible – through the prophets, apostles and New Testament writers have pointed mankind to the truth. Specifically, there are two passages that describe this battle in great clarity. These two passages are both found in the book of Revelation. The first is found in chapter fourteen, verses fourteen through twenty. This passage by itself could lead to some misunderstanding of what John was witnessing. However, when compared to Revelation 19:11-21, we understand exactly what is taking place.

First, in Revelation 14:14-20, John writes,

> *"I looked, and there before me was a white cloud, and seated on the cloud was one 'like a son of man' with a crown of gold on his head and a sharp sickle in his hand. Then another angel came out of the temple and called in a loud voice to him who was sitting on the cloud, 'Take your sickle and reap, because the time to reap has come, for the harvest of the earth is ripe'. So he who was seated on the cloud swung his sickle over the earth, and the earth*

was harvested. Another angel came out of the temple in heaven, and he too had a sharp sickle. Still another angel, who had charge of the fire, came from the altar and called in a loud voice to him who had the sharp sickle, 'Take your sharp sickle and gather the clusters of grapes from the earth's vine, because its grapes are ripe'. The angel swung his sickle on the earth, gathered its grapes and threw them into the great winepress of God's wrath. They were trampled in the winepress outside the city and blood flowed out of the press, rising as high as the horses' bridles for a distance of 1,600 stadia."

In verse fourteen, one "like a son of man with a crown of gold on his head" identifies Jesus Christ as the one who is in charge of this awesome execution of divine Judgment (Rev. 1:13, Daniel 7:13, Mark 8:31). In verse fifteen the angel announces God's perfect timing, for the Day of Judgment has come. Verse sixteen, "he who was seated on the cloud" further re-emphasizes Jesus has been given authority of all judgment (John 5:22, John 12:31, John 16:8-11). Some believe this verse speaks of the "rapture," or gathering of believers. This certainly could be – but the major point is still – Christ is in charge of this "harvest."

In verses seventeen and eighteen, two other angels are seen – one comes out of the temple with a sharp sickle – the other has charge of fire from the altar in the temple. The one with the sharp sickle is instructed by the one who has charge of the fire, "take your sharp sickle and gather the clusters of grapes from the earth's vine, because its grapes are ripe." The perfect timing of God's plan of execution of His judgment is seen here. Also, fire is closely associated with judgment (Revelation 8:3-5, Matthew 18:8, Luke 9:54, 2 Thessalonians 1:7). The sharp sickle is possibly the smaller pruning knife that would allow the "gardener" to cut away clusters in harvest time. True to his word, Jesus said that He would separate the sheep and the goats in Matthew 25:31-33.

In verse nineteen, the angel swings the sickle, gathers the grapes and throws them into the great winepress of God's wrath. In the Old Testament, treading of grapes was used as picture of the execution of divine judgment. If verse sixteen is the opening event – the "gathering of the righteous," this is certainly the closing event – the "winepress of God's wrath." Hear the finality of verse twenty,

> *"They were trampled in the winepress outside the city, and blood flowed out of the press, rising as high as the horses' bridles for a distance of 1,600 stadia."*

First, grapes do not produce blood. Therefore, we realize this symbolic language is speaking of people. Secondly, the phrase "outside the city" points out the fact that bloodshed would defile God's chosen city of Jerusalem (Joel 3:12-14, Hebrews 13:12, Zechariah 14:1-4). Thirdly, what a massive "body count" and loss of human life! All because these people chose to believe a lie rather than acknowledging and receiving God's perfect gift of salvation – His Son Jesus Christ! The distance of 1,600 stadia is about 180 miles! The blood flowed as high as the horses' bridles for 180 miles!

In John's companion passage on the subject, Revelation 19:11-21, we gain better understanding of this awesome event that closes this phase of God's holy and righteous judgment. Let's begin with verses 11-16. John writes,

> *"I saw heaven standing open and there before me was a white horse, whose rider is called Faithful and True. With justice he judges and makes war. His eyes are like blazing fire, and on his head are many crowns. He has a name written on him that no one knows but he himself. He is dressed in a robe dipped in blood, and his name is the Word of God. The armies of heaven were following him, riding on white horses and dressed in fine linen, white and clean. Out of his mouth comes a sharp sword with which to strike down the nations. He will rule them with an iron*

scepter. He treads the winepress of the fury of the wrath of God Almighty. On his robe and on his thigh he has the name written: KING OF KINGS AND LORD OF LORDS."

In this first section of this scene, we see several important truths. One, the rider on the white horse is Jesus Christ (Matthew 3:16, Revelation 3:14, Isaiah 11:1-5, Psalm 96). His eyes blazing, His head adorned with many crowns, a name written on Him (Revelation 1:7, 14; 2:18, 6:2). He is dressed in a robe dipped in blood, and his name is the Word of God (John 1:1, Isaiah 53:5, 63:2).

Secondly, he has the "armies of heaven following Him, riding on white horses and dressed in fine linen, white and clean." Who is this army? His faithful followers (Revelation 3:4, 17:14, 19:8).

Thirdly, He comes with purpose, the purpose of Divine Judgment. A sharp sword comes out of His mouth to strike down the nations (Revelation 1:16, 2:27, 12:5, Psalm 2:9, 2 Thessalonians 2:8). "He treads the winepress of the fury of the wrath of God Almighty" (Revelation 14:20).

Lastly, "On his robe and on his thigh he has this name written: KING OF KINGS AND LORD OF LORDS" (1Timothy 6:15, Revelation 17:14, Philippians 2:6-11). Our God has done all that is needed to demonstrate His love for the world. Verse sixteen reveals, beyond any doubt, the identity of the one riding on the white horse ... the one who is coming in the clouds!

The Battle Scene

In verses 17-21, John describes the battle itself. Beginning in 19:17,

> *"And I saw an angel standing in the sun, who cried in a loud voice to all the birds flying in midair, 'Come, gather together for the great supper of God, so that you may eat the flesh of kings, generals, and mighty men, of horses and their riders, and the flesh of all people, free and slave, small and great'. Then I saw the beast and the kings of the earth and their armies gathered together to make war against the rider on the horse and his army. But the beast was captured and with him the false prophet who had performed the miraculous signs on his behalf. With these signs he had deluded those who had received the mark of the beast and worshipped his image. The two of them were thrown alive into the fiery lake of burning sulfur. The rest of them were killed with the sword that came out of the mouth of the rider on the horse, and all the birds gorged themselves on their flesh."*

The angel in verse seventeen is calling to the vultures to gather for the "great supper of God." This is a stark contrast to the "wedding supper of the Lamb" (Revelation 19:9). The first "supper of God" has finality written all over it. These people of verse eighteen will not only be defeated, their flesh given to the birds to eat, but they will also be eternally separated from their loving Creator. Compare that horrible reality with the folks at the "wedding supper of the Lamb" where the eternal joy and total fulfillment has just begun. Living out – walking, talking, celebrating, worshipping – in the presence of God – forever!! As you read this, what is your choice? Honestly, I hope by this point, it's a no-brainer! Choose Jesus while you can!

Verse nineteen tells us of the opponents for this battle: the beast, the kings of the earth and their armies. These have gathered together to make war against the rider on the white horse and his army (Revelation 16:12-16). In verse twenty, the impending battle is interrupted with the capture of the beast and false prophet with both of them being tossed alive into the eternal fiery lake of burning sulfur (Revelation 20:10, 14, 15; 21:18). Yet, in verse twenty-one, their armies do not escape either! They are killed by the "sword that came out of the mouth of the rider on the horse" – the Word of the Living God! That should answer once and for all – about any doubts of the power of God's Holy Word! Then the birds that were introduced in verse seventeen fulfill their purpose of "cleaning up" by "gorging themselves on their flesh."

You may ask, "Where is Satan during this time of battle?" Does he escape? Is he beyond the reach of God's judgment? Let's look in revelation 20:1-3 for the answer. John writes,

> *"And I saw an angel coming down out of heaven, having the key to the abyss and holding in his hand a great chain. He seized the dragon, that ancient serpent, who is the devil, or Satan, and bound him for a thousand years. He threw him into the Abyss, and locked and sealed it over him, to keep him from deceiving the nations anymore until the thousand years were ended. After that, he must be set free for a short time* (Revelation 1:18, 12:9; Luke 8:31; Matthew 4:10; Isaiah 24:22; 2 Peter 2:4).

With Satan bound, what's next on God's awesome calendar?

The 1,000-Year Reign of Jesus Christ

John speaks to this subject in Revelation 20:4-6. The apostle writes,

> *"I saw thrones on which were seated those who had been given authority to judge. And I saw the souls of those who had been beheaded*

because of their testimony for Jesus and because of the word of God. They had not worshipped the beast or his image and had not received his mark on their foreheads or their hands. They came to life and reigned with Christ a thousand years (The rest of the dead did not come to life until the thousand years were ended). This is the first resurrection. Blessed and holy are those who have part in the first resurrection. The second death has no power over them, but they will be priests of God and of Christ and will reign with him for a thousand years."

In verse four, John sees seats of authority for all those who overcome and stay faithful to the end (Revelation 2:26). He sees the beheaded souls of those who gave their lives for Christ – they come to life and reign with Jesus for a thousand years (Revelation 22:5). In verse five, "the rest of the dead" or the wicked who have died – do not come to life. John defines this as the first resurrection – which is for believers (Matthew 24:31, 1 Corinthians 15:23, 1 Thessalonians 4:16-17, John 5:29, Acts 24:15, Daniel 12:2). In verse six, "Blessed and holy are those who have part in the first resurrection." Who are these who take part in the first resurrection? Those who love and believe in Jesus Christ - in other words - ALL believers - "They will be priests of God and of Christ and reign with him for a thousand years."

Revelation 5:8-10 agrees, this passage is when the Lamb takes the scroll. John writes,

> *"And when he had taken it, the four living creatures and the twenty-four elders fell down before the Lamb. Each one had a harp and they were holding golden bowls full of incense, which are the prayers of the saints. And they sang a new song: You are worthy to take the scroll and to open its seals, because you were slain and with your blood you purchased men for God from every tribe and language and people and nation. You have made them to be a kingdom and priests to serve our God, and they will reign on the earth."*

The prophet Daniel further confirms this truth. Daniel 7:27,

> *"Then the sovereignty, power and greatness of the kingdoms under the whole heaven will be handed over to the saints, the people of the Most High"* (Daniel 7:13-14).

Isaiah describes the celebration in Isaiah 25:6-9,

"On this mountain the Lord Almighty will prepare a feast of rich food for all peoples, a banquet of aged wine – the best meats and the finest of wines. On this mountain he will destroy the shroud that enfolds all peoples, the sheet that covers all nations; He will swallow up death forever. The Sovereign Lord will wipe away the tears from all faces; he will remove the disgrace of his people from all the earth. The Lord has spoken. In that day they will say, 'Surely this is our God; we trusted in him and he saves us. This is the Lord, we trust in him; let us rejoice and be glad in his salvation."

This thousand-year reign of Christ will be the most peaceful, prosperous and glorious time in the history of mankind (Isaiah 2:1-5, 9:6-7, 11:5-12; Jeremiah 23:5-6; Joel 2:32; Amos 9:11-12). There will be no more "wars, rumors of wars, nation against nation, kingdom versus kingdom!" There will be no more famine, pestilence nor wickedness as Jesus rules over the entire earth from his Holy hill in Jerusalem (Jeremiah 3:17, Zechariah 8:3).

This wonderful period closes with one last attempt of Satanic overthrow. John writes in Revelation 20:7-10,

"When the thousand years are over, Satan will be released from his prison and will go out to

deceive the nations in the four corners of the
earth – Gog and Magog – to gather them for
battle. In number they are like the sand on the
seashore. They marched across the camp of
God's people, the city he loves. But fire came
down from heaven and devoured them. And
the devil, who deceived them, was thrown into
the lake of burning sulfur, where the beast and
the false prophet had been thrown. They will
be tormented day and night for ever and
ever."

A good question concerning verse seven, "Why would God release Satan from the Abyss?" I wondered about that as I studied this text for years. The answer is simple – all the people who are born in the Millennial reign live without temptation! They have to be tempted and tested just like every person from every age of human history. What I marvel at is, "Why would anyone, who lives during the earthly reign of Jesus Christ – with all of the peace and prosperity – want to follow anyone else, much less Satan?" Well, the devil draws another crowd of followers "... in number they are like the sand on the seashore." This battle for which they gather is most anti-climatic. As they surround Jerusalem fire falls from heaven and devours them. Satan is then thrown in the "lake of burning sulfur where the beast and the false prophet are." This close of Christ's thousand-year reign sets the stage for God's next great event.

The Great White Throne Judgment

As we look in Revelation 20:11-15, we notice three important truths. One, this judgment is for the wicked only. In verse five of this chapter we learned that,

> *"The rest of the dead did not come to life until*
> *the thousand years were ended."*

Thus, verse five identifies these as the "wicked dead." Believers have already taken "part in the first resurrection" (verse six). The Great White Throne Judgment is, therefore, the second resurrection. Daniel 12:2 confirms,

> *"Multitudes who sleep in the dust of the earth*
> *will awake: some to everlasting life, others to*
> *shame and contempt."*

The phrase "some to everlasting life" is the first resurrection and the phrase "others to shame and contempt" is the second resurrection.

The second truth this judgment is based "on the books" – the Book of Life and the book of records (actions) (verses twelve and fifteen). Some companion verses are: Exodus 32:32; Deuteronomy 29:20; Daniel 12:1; Malachi 3:16; Luke 10:20; Revelation 3:5, 21:27.

First, because their name is NOT found in the Book of Life – Jesus is NOT their Savior. Therefore, these people are now judged solely on "what they had done as recorded in the books" (verse 12b). Thus, their recorded actions, or good works, are not enough to have their sins forgiven! In essence, they must flee (as earth and sky did) from God's presence. There is no place for them, as they are eternally under the curse of sin.

Thirdly, this judgment is final. "The lake of fire is the second death" (verse 14b). This judgment is also "all encompassing" – "the dead, great and small." These people were retrieved from the "sea, death and Hades." Key word here is "death" – thus meaning all of the wicked dead. It does not matter whether they were rich, famous or how they died. All of the wicked will appear at the Great White Throne Judgment!

Let's read the text again, hopefully with new insight. Revelation 20:11-15,

> "Then I saw a great white throne and him who was seated on it. Earth and sky fled from his presence, and there was no place for them. And I saw the dead, great and small, standing before the throne, and the books were opened. Another book was opened, which is the Book of Life. The dead were judged according to what they had done as recorded in the books.

The sea gave up the dead that were in it and death and Hades gave up the dead that were in them, and each person was judged according to what he had done. Then death and Hades were thrown into the lake of fire. The lake of fire is the second death. If anyone's name was not found written in the Book of Life, he was thrown into the lake of fire."

A New Heaven and a New Earth

At the close of Revelation 20:15, we see all evil finally disposed. Satan, the beast, the false prophet, every evil person from every generation – even death and Hades, all thrown into the lake of fire. What's next? That is a great question!

With the awesome beauty of Revelation chapters 21-22, I believe they need no explanation. Therefore, look into these passages and experience the "heart of God." Beginning in Revelation 21:1-8,

"Then I saw a new heaven and a new earth, for the first heaven and the first earth had passed away, and there was no longer any sea. I saw the Holy City, the new Jerusalem, coming down out of heaven from God, prepared as a bride beautifully dressed for her husband. And

*I heard a loud voice from the throne saying,
'Now the dwelling of God is with men, and He
will live with them. They will be His people,
and God Himself will be with them and be
their God. He will wipe every tear from their
eyes. There will be no more death or mourning
or crying or pain, for the old order of things
has passed away'. He who was seated on the
throne said, 'I am making everything new!'
Then he said, 'Write this down, for these words
are trustworthy and true'. He said to me: 'It is
done. I am the Alpha and the Omega, the
Beginning and the End. To him who is thirsty I
will give drink without cost from the spring of
the water of life. He who overcomes will
inherit all this, and I will be his God and he
will be my son. But the cowardly, the
unbelieving, the vile, the murderers, the
sexually immoral, those who practice magic
arts, the idolaters and all liars – their place
will be in the fiery lake of burning sulfur. This
is the second death."*

Now, allow yourself to embrace the beauty and splendor of
the "City of God." We look into Revelation 21:10-22:5, John writes,

"And he carried me away in the Spirit to a mountain great and high, and showed me the Holy City, Jerusalem, coming down out of heaven from God. It shone with the glory of God, and its brilliance was like that of a very precious jewel, like a jasper, clear as crystal. It had a great, high wall with twelve gates, and with twelve angels at the gates. On the gates were written the names of the twelve tribes of Israel. There were three gates on the east, three on the north, three on the south and three on the west. The wall of the city had twelve foundations, and on them were the names of the twelve apostles of the Lamb.

The angel who talked with me had a measuring rod of gold to measure the city, its gates and its walls. The city was laid out like a square, as long as it was wide. He measured the city with the rod and found it to be 12,000 stadia (1,400 miles) in length, and as wide and high as it is long. He measured its wall and it was 144 cubits (200 feet) thick, by man's measurement, which the angel was using. The wall was made of jasper, and the city of pure gold, as pure as glass. The foundations of the city walls were decorated with every kind of precious stone. The first found was jasper, the second sapphire, the third chalcedony, the fourth emerald, the fifth sardonyx, the sixth carnelian, the seventh chrysolite, the eight beryl, the ninth topaz, the tenth chryoprase, the eleventh jacinth and the twelfth amethyst. The twelve gates were twelve pearl, each gate made of a single pearl. The great street of the city was of pure gold, like transparent glass.

I did not see a temple in the city because the Lord God Almighty and the Lamb are its temple. The city does not need the sun or the moon to shine on it, for the glory of God gives it light, and the Lamb is its lamp. The nations will walk by its light, and the kings of the earth will bring their splendor into it. On no day will its gates ever be shut, for there is no night there. The glory and honor of the nations will be brought into it. Nothing impure will ever enter it, nor will anyone who does what is shameful or deceitful, but only those whose names are written in the Lamb's Book of Life.

Then the angel showed me the river of the water of life, as clear as crystal, flowing from the throne of God and of the Lamb down the middle of the great street of the city. On each side of the river stood the tree of life, bearing twelve crops of fruit, yielding its fruit every month. And the leaves of the tree are for the healing of the nations. No longer will there be any curse. The throne of God and of the Lamb will be in the city, and his servants will serve him. They will see His face, and His name will be on their foreheads. There will be no more night. They will not need the light of a lamp or the light of the sun, for the Lord God will give them light. And they will reign for ever and ever."

Daniel saw a glimpse of this awesome truth some five hundred years before John.

Daniel 7:18 reads:

"But the saints of the Most High will receive the kingdom and will possess it forever – yes, forever and ever."

CHAPTER 12

A TIME TO BE ENCOURAGED,

CHALLENGED, AND COMFORTED

A t this point, now that you have received this information from God's Word, the question leaps out – "Where do I go from here?" If you are one who does not know Jesus Christ personally – as both Lord and Savior, please allow me to encourage you to do three things.

One, accept God's provision for your salvation – the Jesus Christ of the Bible. Accept Him now by inviting Him into your life today – DO NOT DELAY. The writer of Hebrews points out in Hebrews 9:27-28,

> *"Just as man is destined to die once, and after that to face judgment, so Christ was sacrificed once to take away the sins of many people; and will appear a second time, not to bear sin, but to bring salvation to those who are waiting for him"* (Romans 5:12-17).

Jesus said in John 5:22-23,

> *"Moreover, the Father judges no one, but has entrusted all judgment to the Son, that all may honor the Son just as they honor the Father. He who does not honor the Son does not honor the Father, who sent him."*

You may not live to see the "rapture" and end-time events." You need to be ready NOW! Luke writes in Acts 17:30b-31,

> *"... but now he commands all people everywhere to repent. For He has set a day when He will judge the world by justice by the man He has appointed. He has given proof of this to all men by raising him from the dead."*

For further reference, use (what is called by many) "The Roman Road" (Romans 3:23, 6:23, 10:9-13). Make your decision today, as Joshua said to the children of Israel in Joshua 24:14-15,

> *"Now fear the Lord and serve Him with all faithfulness. Throw away the gods your forefathers worshipped beyond the River and in Egypt, and serve the Lord. But if serving the Lord seems undesirable to you, then choose for yourselves this day whom you will serve,*

whether the gods your forefathers served
beyond the River, or the gods of the Amorites,
in whose land you are living. But as for me and
my household, we will serve the Lord."

Secondly, after receiving God's provision of salvation, make a commitment to talking with Him (prayer) and reading His Word daily. By doing these two vital things, you will begin to deepen your relationship with Him. Some great Bible passages that will help develop this new relationship are: Deuteronomy 4:7; 2 Chronicles 7:14; Psalm 32:6, 122:6; Matthew 5:44, 6:5-14; 1 Thessalonians 5:16-18; James 5:13-16; 1 Peter 4:7; Romans 12:12. These should be a great start.

Thirdly, find a solid, biblically grounded church and faithfully attend worship services and study groups. As the New Testament church was founded, the believers fully committed themselves to God this way as seen in Acts 2:42: "They devoted themselves to the apostles teaching and to the fellowship, to the breaking of bread and to prayer." Be faithful, as the writer of Hebrews witnesses,

"Let us hold unswervingly to the hope we
profess, for He who promised is faithful. And
let us consider how we may spur one another
on toward love and good deeds. Let us not give
up meeting together, as some are in the habit

of doing, but let us encourage one another and
all the more as you see the Day approaching."

An Encouraging Word to Believers

I also want to be an encouragement to you as a believer in the Lord Jesus Christ. We live in precarious times, particularly with regard to the near future. Be faithful, watch and be ready for His coming (Matthew 25). Be patient, as James teaches in James 5:7-11,

> *"Be patient, then brothers, until the Lord's coming. See how the farmer waits for the land to yield its valuable crop and how patient he is for the autumn and spring rains. You too, be patient and stand firm, because the Lord's coming is near. Don't grumble against each other, brothers, or you will be judged. The Judge is standing at the door! Brothers, as an example of patience in the face of suffering, take the prophets who spoke in the name of the Lord. As you know, we consider blessed those who have persevered. You have heard of Job's perseverance and have seen what the Lord finally brought about. The Lord is full of compassion and mercy."*

Peter encourages all believers to "live holy and godly lives." 2 Peter 3:9-11 says, "The Lord is not slow in keeping His promise, as some understand slowness. He is patient with you, not wanting anyone to perish, but everyone to come to repentance. But the day of the Lord will come like a thief. The heavens will disappear with a roar; the elements will be destroyed by fire, and the earth and everything in it will be laid bare. Since everything will be destroyed in this way, what kind of people ought you to be? You ought to live holy and godly lives."

Paul teaches in 2 Corinthians 5:9-10,

> *"... so we make it our goal to please Him, whether we are at home in the body or away from it. For we must all appear before the judgment seat of Christ that each one may receive what is due him for the things done while in the body, whether good or bad."*

Paul continues this "good" word of encouragement to believers in the same chapter 2 Corinthians 5:16-19,

> *"So from now on we regard no one from a worldly point of view. Though we once regarded Christ in this way, we do so no longer. Therefore, if anyone is in Christ, he is a new creation; the old has gone; the new has*

come! All this is from God, who reconciled us to himself through Christ and gave us the ministry of reconciliation: that God was reconciling the world to himself in Christ, not counting men's sins against them. And He has committed to us the message of reconciliation."

I sincerely desire to give you who are called to be pastors and preachers, (Ephesians 4:11-13), a most encouraging word. Being a pastor, myself, I know the struggles in ministry today. The loneliness, the questions of one's calling, the constant attacks of fear, doubt, and anxiety – all brought through Satan. These and other situations can be discouraging. Being an effective "under-shepherd" is impossible without the power and anointing of the Holy Spirit. Please receive these passages of scripture as a personal word of comfort and encouragement from the Lord. We begin with Paul's positive challenge to a young pastor name Timothy. 2 Timothy 4:1-8 says,

"In the presence of God and of Jesus Christ, who will judge the living and the dead, and in view of his appearing and his kingdom, I give you this charge: Preach the Word' be prepared in season and out of season; correct, rebuke and encourage – with great patience and

careful instruction. For the time will come when men will not put up with sound doctrine. Instead, to suit their own desires, they will gather around them a great number of teachers to say what their itching ears want to hear. They will turn their ears away from the truth and turn aside to myths. But you, keep your head in all situations, endure hardship, do the work of an evangelist, discharge all the duties of your ministry. For I am already being poured out like a drink offering, and the time has come for my departure. I have fought the good fight, I have finished the race, I have kept the faith. Now there is in store for me the crown of righteousness, which the Lord, the righteous Judge, will award to me on that day – and not only to me, but also to all who have longed for His appearing."

In real estate – the slogan is "location, location, location". In ministry the slogan must be, "faithfulness, faithfulness, faithfulness." Stay faithful to your calling, for it is He who called you. Acts 10:42-43 tells us,

"He commanded us to preach to the people and to testify that He (Jesus Christ) is the one

whom God appointed as judge of the living and the dead. All the prophets testify about him that everyone who believes in him receives forgiveness of sins through his name."

I want to leave you with three keys to effective ministry that the Lord has given me. It is the same three things we share with our congregations. First, develop your personal, intimate relationship with Him. For out of this intimacy will flow His power and blessings through you. Abide in Jesus, as He teaches us in John 15:4-5,

"Remain in me, and I will remain in you. No branch can bear fruit by itself; it must remain in the vine. Neither can you bear fruit unless you remain in me. I am the vine; you are the branches. If a man remains in me and I in him, he will bear much fruit; apart from me you can do nothing."

When we abide in Him – He will grow the church according to His good pleasure and purpose.

Secondly, STAY IN THE WORD! We cannot preach the Word without consistently and persistently studying the Word. Too many preachers and pastors today preach "other" messages rather than God's Holy Word! I learned long ago, people do not need to hear my views and opinions – because they have NO POWER! God's Word is powerful! Again as Paul instructs Timothy in 2 Timothy 3:15b-17,

> "... the holy Scriptures ... are able to make you wise for salvation through faith in Christ Jesus. All Scripture is God-breathed and is useful for teaching, rebuking, correcting and training in righteousness, so that the man of God may be thoroughly equipped for every good work."

1 Corinthians 1:18 reminds us:

> "For the message of the cross is foolishness to those who are perishing, but to us who are being saved it is the power of God."

Therefore, our preaching should be Christ-centered. As the Apostle Paul said,

> "For I resolved to know nothing while I was with you except Jesus Christ and him crucified" (1 Corinthians 2:2).

May this be the deepest heartfelt cry in our ministries, now and always.

Thirdly – delegate, delegate, delegate. No one human being can do all that is needed in any ministry or local church. That is why God gave us spiritual gifts (Ephesians 4:11-16; 1Corintihians 12:1-31; Romans 12:4-7). Study these texts, teach your people these truths, and look for the gifts as they are manifested in each person. Then as you discover individual giftedness and help others to discover their spiritual giftedness – place them in ministry and watch as God grows the "local body." There is no greater joy in ministry than when the body of Christ functions in unity as she is intended to by her Lord.

These three things I have found to be vital in spiritual and church growth. Yet, if we leave out the underlying foundation, we will totally and utterly fail. The foundation for everything is LOVE. Jesus said in John 13:34-35,

> *"A new command I give you: Love one another.*
> *As I have loved you, so you must love one*
> *another. By this all men will know that you*
> *are my disciples, if you love one another."*

In reality, these three keys belong to the third priority in our lives – namely "our" ministries. Our first priority has to be our God – NOT OUR RELIGION! It is all about our relationship with Him. 1 John 4:16b,

"God is love. Whoever lives in love lives in God,
and God in him."

Our second priority in life must be our wives and our children. Ephesians 5:25, "Husbands, love your wives just as Christ loved the church and gave himself up for her."
Our marriages either reflect Jesus Christ to our congregations or they do not. How you and I treat our wives may be the only "Jesus" some will ever witness. Peter warns in 1 Peter 3:7,

"Husbands, in the same way be considerate as
you live with your wives ... so that nothing will
hinder your prayers."

Before you begin to sense too much pressure – remember we cannot accomplish this without Christ. But, Paul says it very well in Philippians 4:13,

"I can do everything through Him who gives
me strength."

Our love of God must be expressed constantly toward our families. Ephesians 6:4 exhorts us,

"Fathers, do not exasperate your children;
instead, bring them up in the training and

instruction of the Lord" (Deuteronomy 4:9, 6:7).

They are a blessing from the Lord. We must love them by helping them on their way to Him (Malachi 4:6, Matthew 19:14, Mark 10:14-16, Luke 18:16). Love is the foundation for our lives as we allow Him to use us as channels of blessings – first to Himself, then our families and thirdly our ministries.

It has been a profound privilege for me to share God's Word through the writing of this book. My prayer is that God will richly bless you – the reader – as you continue to watch, serve and prepare for His coming. 2 Peter 3:10a reminds us,

"But the day of the Lord will come like a thief."

Of course we must let our Lord Jesus have the final word:

"Therefore keep watch because you do not know on what day your Lord will come."

NOTES:

Chapter 2

1. NIV Study Bible, 1995, 10th Anniversary Edition, Zondervan Publishing House, Grand Rapids, Michigan.
2. "Handbook of Today's Religions", Josh McDowell and Don Stewart, 1983, Thomas Nelson Publishers, Nashville, TN.
3. Funk and Wagnall's Standard College Dictionary, 1963, Harcourt, Brace and World, New York.

Chapter 4

1. Webster's II New Riverside Dictionary, 1996, Office edition, Houghton Mifflin Company.
2. NIV Study Bible, 1995, 10th Anniversary Edition, Zondervan Publishing House, Grand Rapids, Michigan.

Chapter 6

1. NIV Study Bible, 1995, 10th Anniversary Edition, Zondervan Publishing House, Grand Rapids, Michigan.
2. NIV Study Bible, 1995, 10th Anniversary Edition, Zondervan Publishing House, Grand Rapids, Michigan
3. Funk and Wagnall's Standard College Dictionary, 1963, Harcourt, Brace and World, New York.

4. "A Survey of the New Testament", Robert H. Gundry, 1970, Zondervan Publishing House, Grand Rapids, Michigan.

Chapter 7

1. "A Survey of the New Testament", Robert H. Gundry, 1970, Zondervan Publishing House, Grand Rapids, Michigan.
2. "The 1980's: The Countdown to Armageddon", Hal Lindsey, 1980, Westgate Press, Inc. King of Prussia, Pennsylvania.
3. "The 1980's: The Countdown to Armageddon", Hal Lindsey, 1980, Westgate Press, Inc. King of Prussia, Pennsylvania.
4. Searchlight Ministries, John Courson, 2005, notes taken during a radio message on Christian Sattelite Network.

Chapter 8

1. NIV Study Bible, 1995, 10th Anniversary Edition, Zondervan Publishing House, Grand Rapids, Michigan.
2. NIV Study Bible, 1995, 10th Anniversary Edition, Zondervan Publishing House, Grand Rapids, Michigan.
3. NIV Study Bible, 1995, 10th Anniversary Edition, Zondervan Publishing House, Grand Rapids, Michigan.
4. NIV Study Bible, 1995, 10th Anniversary Edition, Zondervan Publishing House, Grand Rapids, Michigan.
5. NIV Study Bible, 1995, 10th Anniversary Edition, Zondervan Publishing House, Grand Rapids, Michigan.
6. "A Survey of the New Testament", Robert H. Gundry, 1970, Zondervan Publishing House, Grand Rapids, Michigan.

Chapter 10

1. "The Rapture Question Answered", Robert Van Kampen, 1997, Baker Publishing Group, Ada, Michigan.
2. "The Rapture Question Answered", Robert Van Kampen, 1997, Baker Publishing Group, Ada, Michigan.

Chapter 11

1. 1. NIV Study Bible, 1995, 10th Anniversary Edition, Zondervan Publishing House, Grand Rapids, Michigan.

ABOUT THE AUTHOR

Samuel King graduated from Elon University with a Bachelor of Science Degree in 1976. Surrendering to the call of ministry in 1990, he earned a Master's degree in Religious Education from Southwestern Baptist Theological Seminary in Fort Worth, Texas. Samuel has studied God's Word for more than forty years and has been in pastoral ministry for over twenty-five years.

Samuel founded Walking in the Word Ministries, Inc in 2007. He also pastors a growing church in the metro Richmond area where he lives with his wife, Judith. They have three adult children and one grandchild. He enjoys sports, reading and travel.

Connect with Us on Facebook!

Walking In The Word Ministries Inc.

Made in the USA
Middletown, DE
02 August 2021